SUCCESS
STARTS
TODAY

Most CelebrityPress® titles are available at special quantity discounts for bulk purchases for sales promotions, premiums, fundraising, and educational use. Special versions or book excerpts can also be created to fit specific needs.

For more information, please write:
CelebrityPress®
520 N. Orlando Ave, #2
Winter Park, FL 32789
or call 1.877.261.4930

Visit us online at: www.CelebrityPressPublishing.com

SUCCESS
STARTS
TODAY

CelebrityPress®
Winter Park, Florida

CONTENTS

CHAPTER 1

SUCCESS STARTS NOW
THE TIME TO TAKE ACTION IS RIGHT THIS MOMENT

BY JACK CANFIELD

People don't realize that now is all there ever is; there is no past or future except as memory or anticipation in your mind.
~ Eckhart Tolle

Now is all you have—this very moment. The past is gone and the future hasn't arrived, so the only way you can ever truly experience anything is to focus on the present and live in awareness from one moment to the next.

Of course, this means that NOW is the only time you can ever experience success. Not "soon," not "then," not "later." Now! And it begins with you.

SUCCESS STARTS WITH A DECISION

It begins when you make the decision to create a life filled with whatever "success" means to you. Abundance, happiness, purpose, joy, satisfaction, fulfillment—whatever your dream life looks like, you can decide right now, this very moment, to create it. That decision is the most important step you will ever take toward making your vision a reality.

Not only can you make the decision to create your ideal future now, you can start living it now. The happiness you desire, that sense of abundance, they are available for you to enjoy right now in this moment. You don't have to wait until you achieve some big goal. You can experience more joy and fulfillment immediately—simply by shifting the focus of your thinking from what you DON'T have to what you DO have. Because no matter how far you are from your ideal level of wealth, or how much stuff you have (or think you don't have), I guarantee you have so many more gifts and blessings than you think.

For example, if you're reading this, you have enough money to buy a book. You most likely have a place to live, running water, electricity, a refrigerator with food in it, a cell phone with a camera in it, a computer with access to the Internet, a television, a car or access to Uber, Lyft or public transportation. And if you have access to the Internet, you have Wikipedia at your fingertips – as well as more than 2,400 TED and 40,000 TEDx talks and millions of YouTube videos that you can learn from and be inspired by. You have access to Google, Amazon, iTunes, Pandora, Google Maps, Waze, and more than 2 million other apps that make it easier for you to increase your productivity, add more joy and purpose to your life, and learn everything you could ever want to know about any topic that interests you. How incredible is that?

If you spent just a few minutes every day being grateful for what you have rather than focusing on what you don't have, I guarantee your sense of abundance will increase enormously. The same is true for happiness. You can experience misery or boundless joy at any moment simply by choosing to think negative or positive thoughts. It's always your choice.

If you find yourself thinking thoughts like these:
- "I'll never be successful."
- "I am always going to be alone."
- "Life is unfair."
- "If I ask that person to mentor me, they'll probably say no."
- "I'm never going to be able to lose forty pounds."
... then your thoughts will become a self-fulfilling prophecy and you will end up unhappy. If you believe you will never be successful, you won't be. It's that simple.

The good news is the opposite is true as well. You can just as easily choose to think thoughts that make you happy, such as:
- "I have everything I need to accomplish anything I want."

- "I have so much love in my life."
- "Life always works out for the best."
- "If I ask enough people to mentor me, someone will say yes because I have a lot of potential."
- "I have the will power and the commitment and the access to the resources and the support I need to successfully lose forty pounds."

... once again, your thoughts will become a self-fulfilling prophecy.

As the legendary Henry Ford once said, "Whether you think you can or think you can't – you're right." I encourage you right now to make the choice that will bring you the most happiness and fulfillment.

Don't wait to be successful at some future point. Have a successful relationship with the present moment and be fully present in whatever you are doing. That is success.
~ Eckhart Tolle

IT'S TIME TO STOP THINKING ABOUT DOING IT – AND DO IT

Now is the only time you can choose to take action toward your dreams – so what are you waiting for?

I remember participating in a teleseminar with Jim Bunch, founder and director of The Ultimate Game, a few years back. He had invited several people from the Transpersonal Leadership Council to experience his work for free and I had gladly signed up.

On our first call, Jim asked each of us to share what it was we wanted to achieve from the seminar. When it was my turn, I said that I wanted to lose weight and get fit. Jim said, "Great, let's start now. Put down the phone and do twenty pushups and then pick up the phone again."

"No, that's not what I mean," I told him. "I'm talking about joining a health club, getting a trainer and changing my eating habits."

He said, "I get that, but put down the phone and give me twenty pushups right now."

We went back and forth like this about five times before I finally relented, put down the phone and did twenty pushups. What I learned that day is that talking about it doesn't get it done. Planning it doesn't get it done. DOING it gets it done, and there is magic in beginning it now, without delay or hesitation.

The man who moves a mountain begins by carrying away small stones.
~ Confucius

DON'T LET ANOTHER SECOND PASS YOU BY

My friend Stephen Josephs is an incredibly successful executive coach. When I first met him, we were both graduate students at the University of Massachusetts in Amherst. Stephen was also a yoga instructor at the time. One night, he was at a party where an overweight woman marveled at how thin and fit he looked. She told him, "Oh, I would love to be as thin as you," and asked him for advice on how she could achieve that.

"You can start by putting that cookie down," he suggested.

She laughed and said, "Oh no, I could never do that. I love chocolate too much!"

She had the opportunity to act in that moment and take the first step toward achieving her ideal weight and fitness level, but she chose not to. Every moment we have that choice to begin. To start. If you're like the woman above but actually serious about losing weight, you could begin by removing all the sugar and high-sugar, overly processed food products from your kitchen and pantry. You could get up right this moment and go for a twenty-minute walk. You could choose not to eat after eight o'clock at night. You could decide to stop eating cookies or you could choose to get down and do twenty pushups. All of these actions could be the first step on your journey to your ultimate goal.

THERE'S NO SUCH THING AS THE PERFECT MOMENT

You don't have to get it perfect; you just have to get it going.
~ T. Harv Eker

Most people I meet are waiting for the "perfect moment" to start. It's as if they're looking for a sign, like 12 white doves flying over their house in the formation of a cross, to reveal the perfect time to start. I don't think I have to tell you that's never going to happen!

Yet so many people persist in waiting, and hesitating, and NOT taking action. They just sit around talking about it, saying only that they'll "get around to it someday."

But someday is like "tomorrow" from the musical, *Annie*—it's a day that never truly arrives.

When I was in my twenties, I had the good fortune to work for W. Clement Stone, a very wealthy self-made man. He grew up very poor in Chicago then went on to found the Combined Insurance Company, achieved a net worth of $600 million dollars, became the publisher of Success Magazine, and wrote a book entitled, *The Success System that Never Fails*.

One of Mr. Stone's favorite sayings was, "Do it now." This was such a core part of his philosophy that he printed up a bunch of round wooden coins with the letters TUIT on them. Whenever anyone said they would do something when they "got around to it," he would hand them one of those round wooden coins and say, "There you go! You now have a round *TUIT*, so let's get on with it." I still have one of those round TUITs on my desk.

That message has always stuck with me – and it's why I have been so successful. It's how *Chicken Soup for the Soul*, which has earned me tens of millions of dollars, came into being. In the early 1990s, people began telling me that I should put all of the inspirational stories that I had been using in my talks into a book. Once I made the decision to go for it, I didn't wait for the perfect moment to take action – I just got started. On a flight from Boston back to Los Angeles (where I was living at the time), I made a list of all the great stories I knew and had used in my talks and workshops over the years. There were about 70 of them. I made a decision on that flight to write two stories a week until the book was complete. I started the next night and finished the book in less than a year with the help of Mark Victor Hansen, who contributed thirty of his own favorite stories. The rest, as they say, is history. The *Chicken Soup for the Soul* series has now sold more than five hundred million books around the world.

THE ONLY WAY TO LEARN IT IS TO DO IT

There is nothing wrong with planning, but too much planning and not enough action never works. The best way to learn something is simply to do it. As a wise man once said, "You learn to play the piano by playing the piano." You learn how to be a better parent by being a parent. You learn to be a better teacher by teaching, and a better manager by managing. All you have to do is take action, pay attention to the feedback, and then respond to that feedback.

Every action you take creates a result, and that result is the feedback you need to pay attention to. Did you get the date? Get the sale? Get the job? Get the raise? Make the bestseller list? Get the loan? Hit your target? Did you end up feeling happy, content, fulfilled? If not, what did you learn? How can you apply that feedback to your next action, your next sale, your next venture, your next book?

This is how you learn and get better.

THREE SIMPLE TIPS TO ACCELERATE YOUR MOMENTUM, ONCE YOU TAKE THAT FIRST STEP

After you make your decision and take that first step toward success, what's next? How can you keep yourself moving forward to your goals, even when you hit the inevitable roadblock?

Here are three tips to help you out:

1. Lean into it.
Success happens when you lean into it—when you open yourself to opportunity and are willing to do what it takes to pursue it further, without any expectations or promise of success. You lean into the opportunity, take action, and see what it feels like. And if you find that you want to keep going, you do.

That's how you create momentum and bring more opportunity, resources, and people who can help you into your life—usually at the perfect time for you to benefit from them.

Just be aware that leaning into it means you must be willing to start without seeing the entire journey ahead of you. You must be ready to explore and follow the path through unknown territory without knowing where it leads. Above all, you have to trust that the journey will take you where you want to go—or someplace even better.

2. Follow the Rule of 5.

Lots of people set goals for themselves, and take the first few steps toward achieving those goals – then get stuck because of overwhelm. There are too many things to learn, too many choices to make, too many things to do. And it's easy to get discouraged when you don't feel like you're making the progress you should be making.

That's why I always encourage people to use the "Rule of 5." It's simple: every day, set yourself five specific tasks that will take you closer to your goal. They don't have to be big tasks—I'm talking about reading an article, sending an important email, writing a certain number of words, making a phone call, spending 30 minutes researching a relevant topic, and so on—whatever you can complete in the time you have available that day.

Then, once you have set your five tasks, make sure you complete them before you go to bed that night. It's a simple but very effective way to chunk down your big goal into small, achievable steps and make consistent progress toward your goals. After all, as my friend Ron Scolastico, once told me, "If you go every day to a very large tree and take five swings at it with a very sharp axe, eventually, no matter how large the tree, it's going to come down."

3. Make yourself accountable.

Holding yourself accountable to your commitments is one of the most fundamental and effective traits of a successful person. But it's one thing to be accountable to yourself—and another to be accountable to someone else. When it comes to creating results, two heads are almost always better than one.

That's because success is rarely a solo effort. You will find that you are able to accomplish so much more, faster, if you hold yourself accountable to someone else. This could be an accountability partner or a mastermind group—a person or group with whom you can share your goals and discuss your challenges, and who will cheer you on and support you as you work to achieve your goals. Or you may want to work with a coach or an experienced mentor who will hold you accountable while helping you overcome any blocks or challenges you encounter on your journey.

When you lean into opportunity, set yourself strategic tasks that help you make steady progress toward your goals, and make yourself accountable for completing those tasks, you will be amazed at how much you can accomplish, and how quickly.

Just remember: if you want to succeed, you've got to start now.

NO MATTER WHO OR WHERE YOU ARE, NOW IS THE TIME TO START

You are never too old to set another goal or dream a new dream.
~ C.S. Lewis

One of my favorite stories is about Helen Klein, a woman I met while receiving an "Outstanding Californian" award for having coauthored so many *Chicken Soup for the Soul* books. Helen was in her eighties when I met her—but she looked like she was in her fifties. She was lean and fit, with smooth skin and a disarming smile, and was being honored for her achievements as a runner. She had recently broken the world marathon record in her age group—the 80- to 85-year-old class—and had completed the 26.2-mile run in four hours and 31 minutes! Talk about an inspiring role model.

But Helen hadn't always been lean and fit. When she was fifty-five years old, her husband asked her if she would train with him to run a ten-mile race in a few months. She was an overweight nurse at the time, had been a smoker for twenty-five years, and had never run a mile in her life. That first night, they decided to run laps on a track they marked off in their large back yard. Helen was so out of shape that after two laps around the yard, she was exhausted and panting and thinking she would die. But she decided to give up smoking and to continue running, adding one lap more each day. Ten weeks later she completed the ten-mile race. She finished last, but she had finished. Encouraged by this success, she entered other races and went on to have an amazing career as a runner—despite having started when she was fifty-five.

Here are just a few of her accomplishments, as chronicled by Dan Millman in *Chicken Soup for Body and Soul:*

"At fifty-nine, Helen was the oldest woman in the world to complete the Ironman Triathlon, consisting of a 2.4-mile ocean swim, a 112-mile bike ride, followed immediately by a 26.2-mile run... At age sixty-six, Helen ran five 100-mile mountain trail races within sixteen weeks. In 1991, she ran across the state of Colorado in five days and ten hours, setting the world record for the 500K. She also holds a world age-group record in the 100-mile run, has completed more than sixty marathons and nearly 140 ultramarathons. In 1995, still getting younger, Helen ran 145 miles across the Sahara Desert; in 1995, she completed the 370-mile Eco Challenge, running with Team Operation Smile."

In the Echo Challenge, Helen "rode thirty-six miles on horseback; hiked ninety miles through the broiling desert heat; negotiated eighteen miles through freezing water–filled canyons; mountain biked thirty miles; rappelled down a 440-foot cliff; climbed 1,200 feet straight up; paddled ninety miles on a river raft; hiked another twenty miles; and, finally, canoed fifty miles to the finish line."

Helen Klein is proof that it's never too late to start—and that it's okay to start slow and steady, knowing that every step you take will bring you closer to your goal.

NOW IT'S YOUR TURN

It's time for you to take action. Right this moment, you have a decision to make: are you going to take that first step toward creating the life of your dreams?

Are you ready to make it happen?

If your answer is yes, here's what you need to do. Take a moment right this second to write down five tasks you will complete in the next 24 hours that will bring you closer to your ideal reality.

These don't have to be big tasks. They don't have to be hard, or take a lot of time.

You could choose to:
- Create a list of 3 to 5 topics you'd like to learn more about
- Create a list of 3 to 5 articles you'd like to read to learn more about one of your main topics of interest
- Send an email to someone who can help you achieve one of your goals
- Ask someone for feedback that will help you improve your performance in some area of your life
- Create your "Rule of 5" list for tomorrow
- Commit to spending 5 to 10 minutes visualizing what you want tomorrow to look like – right before you go to bed
- Tell 1 to 3 people you love them
- Raise your vibration by spending 10 minutes listing everything you're grateful for in your life
- Make the decision to start consciously reframing your negative thoughts as positive ones
- Make a small but important commitment to your health—e.g., walking for at least 10 minutes a day, no more eating after 8 pm, or no processed foods for a week

The choice is up to you. They can be any small actions you like, but they must bring you closer to your goals in some way.

Create that list right now. Go ahead—I'll still be here when you get back. Are you back? Did you create your list? Great! Now make the commitment to complete those five tasks in the next 24 hours—and you will have taken a huge step closer to your dreams.

THE MOMENT YOU COMMIT, THE UNIVERSE COMMITS TO YOU

I'd like to leave you with the following passage from William Hutchinson Murray's book, *The Scottish Himalayan Expedition*:

Until one is committed, there is hesitancy, the chance to draw back. Concerning all acts of initiative (and creation), there is one elementary truth that ignorance of which kills countless ideas and splendid plans: that the moment one definitely commits oneself, then Providence moves too. All sorts of things occur to help one that would never otherwise have occurred. A whole stream of events issues from the decision, raising in one's favor all manner of unforeseen incidents and meetings and material assistance, which no man could have dreamed would have come his way... Whatever you can do, or dream you can do, begin it. Boldness has genius, power, and magic in it. Begin it now.

Begin. Right now. Just begin. It's probably the greatest success secret I know. I encourage you to look deep into your heart and ask yourself what you truly want—and always remember that NOW is the time to take action and make it happen.

About Jack

Known as America's #1 Success Coach, Jack Canfield is the CEO of the Canfield Training Group in Santa Barbara, CA, which trains and coaches entrepreneurs, corporate leaders, managers, sales professionals and the general public in how to accelerate the achievement of their personal, professional and financial goals.

Jack Canfield is best known as the coauthor of the #1 New York Times bestselling *Chicken Soup for the Soul®* book series, which has sold more than 500 million books in 47 languages, including 11 New York Times #1 bestsellers. As the CEO of Chicken Soup for the Soul Enterprises he helped grow the *Chicken Soup for the Soul®* brand into a virtual empire of books, children's books, audios, videos, CDs, classroom materials, a syndicated column and a television show, as well as a vigorous program of licensed products that includes everything from clothing and board games to nutraceuticals and a successful line of Chicken Soup for the Pet Lover's Soul® cat and dog foods.

His other books include *The Success Principles™: How to Get from Where You Are to Where You Want to Be* (recently revised as the 10th Anniversary Edition), *The Success Principles for Teens, The Aladdin Factor, Dare to Win, Heart at Work, The Power of Focus: How to Hit Your Personal, Financial and Business Goals with Absolute Certainty, You've Got to Read This Book, Tapping into Ultimate Success, Jack Canfield's Key to Living the Law Attraction,* his recent novel, *The Golden Motorcycle Gang: A Story of Transformation* and *The 30-Day Sobriety Solution.*

Jack is a dynamic speaker and was recently inducted into the National Speakers Association's Speakers Hall of Fame. He has appeared on more than 1000 radio and television shows including Oprah, Montel, Larry King Live, the Today Show, Fox and Friends, and 2 hour-long PBS Specials devoted exclusively to his work. Jack is also a featured teacher in 12 movies including *The Secret, The Meta-Secret, The Truth, The Keeper of the Keys, Tapping into the Source,* and *The Tapping Solution.* Jack was also honored recently with a documentary that was produced about his life and teachings, "The Soul of Success: The Jack Canfield Story".

Jack has personally helped hundreds of thousands of people on six different continents become multi-millionaires, business leaders, best-selling authors, leading sales professionals, successful entrepreneurs, and world-class athletes while at the same time creating balanced, fulfilling and healthy lives.

His corporate clients have included Virgin Records, SONY Pictures, Daimler-Chrysler, Federal Express, GE, Johnson & Johnson, Merrill Lynch, Campbell's Soup, Re/Max, The Million Dollar Forum, The Million Dollar Roundtable, The Young Entrepreneurs

Organization, The Young Presidents Organization, the Executive Committee, and the World Business Council.

He is the founder of the Transformational Leadership Council and a member of Evolutionary Leaders, two groups devoted to helping create a world that works for everyone.

Jack is a graduate of Harvard, earned his M.Ed. from the University of Massachusetts and has received three honorary doctorates in psychology and public service. He is married, has three children, two step-children and a grandson.

For more information, visit:
- www.JackCanfield.com
- www.CanfieldTraintheTrainer.com

CHAPTER 2

BURNT OUT?

HOW RECAPTURING LIFE'S JOY AND INTENTION CHANGED MY LIFE

BY DR. VEERLE VAN TRICHT

If you're burnt out you are likely suffering in all areas of your life, but this is not necessary. You do have the power to transform and rise above it.

It's inevitable. Busy people tend to be focused too much in one area or try to be everything to all people. They keep going and going until they find themselves staring foggy- minded at a massive wall—a wall they no longer feel they can conquer. It's tall and daunting and feels, well, helpless. You just cannot do anymore at that moment. You're burnt out and you need help.

I'll never forget when I experienced this moment. It was so awful and quite lonely despite knowing that I was loved by my family and a successful, respected eye surgeon with more money than time to spend it. I had just had my first child and was trying to master motherhood with the same vigour I'd mastered being an eye surgeon. When I learned that the professional demands of my life didn't take my new adventure into motherhood into account I was shocked. They want me back to work full time in two weeks … really? In my heart and mind, I simply was not ready. But with no other choices that I could see, I did it. What a struggle it was, one that I carried with me every day and wrestled with every night—even when I was supposed to be spending time with my precious baby.

The day came when I could not take any more of it. I was burnt out and the downward spiral my life had become was emotionally painful. I felt like I was losing and failing. Nothing could stop it. Despite helping others see through the work I do, I had not allowed myself to see my reality.

I knew something had to change so I stepped back and evaluated my life as a whole, all parts of it, really, and began to search for answers that could not be found in my medical textbooks. Through all of it, I saw a solution with clarity that would take me from the downward spiral into an upward lift.

Because of this I was able to see success in smaller pieces that define my life overall. I was so excited and when I put all this information together it worked. It actually worked! And a new passion was ignited, that of holistic mentor and coach. Today, I have more time, energy, and balance in my life than ever before. I know how to be good for me so I can be good as a surgeon, mother, partner, and coach to others. I've even created the Burnout Resuscitation Program© with all I've learned, so I can help anyone who is teetering on burnout or already there make the changes that help them reclaim their joyous lives. This provides me with joy beyond what words can describe.

THIRTEEN RISK FACTORS OF BURNOUT

When western medicine let me down in my pursuit of solutions, I knew that it was a new calling in my life to help others realize the symptoms of burnout taking hold in their lives.

The sources of burnout can be broken down into three categories: health, mind and personality, and external (environmental) factors. All thirteen of the risk factors fall into these categories and some cross over into two categories due to their nature. As you read each one, take a few moments to reflect on your life. Even if you only have a few of these factors taking place in your life, it's enough to escalate your chances of experiencing burnout and the challenges that come with it.

1. <u>A suppressed immune system</u>: this can lead to repetitive colds, depression, a higher risk of certain cancers, and other infections, as well as autoimmune diseases.

2. Exhaustion and chronic fatigue: overdoing it with all life's obligations without focusing on proper rest can lead to this. However, there is one other thing that surprises many people, and that is the presence of heavy metal in your body. These can be found in lipstick, deodorant, and the environment around you. When I was suffering from exhaustion I got all mercury fillings removed from my teeth and it made a tremendous difference in my energy level.

3. Insufficient levels of vitamins and minerals: choosing too much fast food (which lacks sufficient nutrients) over organic food or raw unprocessed food can deplete vitamin and mineral levels in the body. Excessive stress and alcohol consumption also deplete vitamins D and B as well as magnesium when you need it the most.

4. Drug abuse and certain prescriptions: while antibiotics can be life-saving, they can also lessen your immune system and increase your chances of developing food allergies or having excess fluid in your system. While I've never struggled with addiction, I know the devastation that this causes a person in all areas of their life.

5. Being a control freak: if this statement is reflective of you, you likely have some control issues: "As long as everything is exactly the way I want it, I'm totally flexible." This type of obsession about being in control can lead to anxiety and burnout.

6. Life changes: a certain amount of change is exciting and stimulating, but some change can be stressful and become a catalyst for burnout. For example—your employer being bought out by another business, job change, moving, divorce, marriage, the loss of a loved one, the birth of a child.

7. Inability to cope: when life's responsibilities become too much we can often shut down and begin the process of burnout. This happens when you are managing bills, a career, parenting, daily stress, and anxiety. It can also lead to adrenal malfunction and fatigue, which can make an already tough situation even worse.

8. Hormonal changes: both men and women can experience hormonal changes. For men, it may have to do with ageing and activity levels. For women, it could be those things plus physical changes from pregnancy. The result is a disruptive change in the hypothalamic-pituitary-adrenal axis causing a plethora of physical havoc.

9. Lack of sleep: the body and mind require sleep every night to recharge and prepare us to go about our days with the proper amount of energy. If you have an unhealthy sleep environment or have too

much electronic stimulation near bedtime you likely aren't sleeping as soundly – or as much – as you need to.

10. Being a workaholic: it is impossible to have balance in your life and be good to yourself and your relationships when all you do is work. Eventually, something will break.

11. Being a people pleaser: when you continually say "yes" to others, you are likely saying "no" to yourself and depriving yourself of "me time."

12. Drama in relationships: some drama is caused by burnout and burnout can also lead to drama, so you really have to be careful about this. Try not to have a short fuse and a temper that you unleash upon those you need (your support team.)

13. Sleep disruption: this is something that is a big concern to people who work night shifts and also new parents who find themselves having to get up every few hours to tend to their sweet little bundles of love.

By not being aware of how we treat ourselves we are all likely to have touches with many of these burnout risks. It's important to your health and emotional wellbeing to find ways to create a centered lifestyle that helps you achieve the successes that you desire in your professional and personal life.

TEETERING ON THE EDGE

These are the warning signs that you are teetering on the edge of burnout.

One of my greatest successes with the Burnout Resuscitation Program© comes with the educational component. It has allowed me a platform to show people who are on the edge that they are actually there. Because of this, many have caught themselves before full burnout. And those who have, find themselves with renewed hope and the required energy to change their life's course. This is so rewarding! You see, the medical community doesn't officially recognize burnout, despite it being a highly common, global problem.

The most vulnerable people to experience burnout in today's high demand world are those professionals who have children and struggle to balance all their roles.

Think about your life, or the life of someone you care about. If they are experiencing any of the symptoms below, they are experiencing a burnout symptom. It may be hard to say, or even admit, but if this is you, something needs to change:

- Terrible exhaustion that just does not go away.
- Lying awake at night, worrying mainly about money and its perceived relevance in your life. During these times, you convince yourself that you must keep on going on unhappy about your job and life in general, in order to provide materially for everyone else.
- Not taking time to recharge. When you deny yourself precious "me time" and give, give, give, you are depleting yourself emotionally, mentally, and physically.
- Bickering and fighting in your relationships is more common, creating a wedge that separates you and your partner. This is when you need a partner most—to help you and support you and your needs. And your partner needs you there for them too!
- You just don't like your job any longer. You once did, but now it's a burden. The thought of it irritates you and you find that you are setting yourself up for bad days more than good days at work.

Do any of these symptoms linger in your life? I used to brush mine away and ignore them...until I no longer could. Thankfully, these symptoms are not symbolic of the way it has to be. You can move beyond them.

SIX STEPS TO ELIMINATING BURNOUT FOREVER

Eliminating stress and increasing energy levels opens up the passion and joy for life that you once had—and likely miss. You can make life-altering choices by investing into the life that you are meant to live.

My journey from burnout to bursting with passion took me over a decade to complete. There simply were no resources out there to help me through the process so it took my medical mind merging with my spiritual necessity to find the right balance. Once it began to guide me, I saw amazing transformations begin to unfold. It felt so good, and so freeing. I was finally able to be a better mother, even a stronger doctor, a better partner, and a more joyful participant in life in general.

The clients that I work with as a coach today are beautiful, daily reminders that whoever we are or what circumstances we find ourselves in, there is hope for us. No one is destined to live burnt out for as long as it'll carry them. We are all designed to have intricate life experiences that are filled with many emotions, challenges, and joys. With some help, we can handle these in the most graceful manner possible. These steps guide us to that point:

1. <u>Time Creator</u>: at times, burnout can be so intense that it becomes life threatening. During this first step, you will find the ways to create the time you need in order to begin your journey back to health and joy. In turn, you are able to find more quality time in which to be healthier for others, as well.

2. <u>Energy Booster</u>: in order to boost your energy, you will learn techniques such as a daily gratitude ritual, power walking, manifestation, and boundaries and protections to help you regain control of a balanced and engaged life. The component of wellness is also addressed through learning what types of foods can be consumed to help. I have an amazing smoothie recipe that I drink every morning that fuels my entire day!

3. <u>Find Your Life Purpose</u>: through connecting with you hidden talents you can ignite a passion that helps you to live your life purpose and also connect with your soul purpose. We all want to do what we love! I love being a surgeon and being a coach to help others.

4. <u>The Love Shack</u>: by learning what your "love language" is, you are able to connect with the approaches, words, and outcomes that keep your relationships stronger and healthier. You are able to generate responses that match in others through this positive energy (also known as positive vibrations).

5. <u>Wheel of Life</u>: in order to live an engaged life, you need balance in all areas of it. Through learning how you can make this type of balance a lifestyle choice that serves your purpose, and even a greater good, you will grow more aware of when things are off-kilter so you can take action before it is too late.

6. <u>Connect with Your Higher Consciousness for Unlimited Possibilities of Growth</u>: when we don't listen to our higher consciousness, we

start to defy the choices that are right for us to make and which resonate from within us. This is how we prevent burnout. My higher consciousness is a trusted source that is pure and with good intention, as is yours.

Burnout does not have to come with the territory of "success" and "busyness." You do have options on how to become alert to the symptoms in your own life. It's a powerful and lovely day when you can look at yourself in the mirror and see the joy and excitement you once had returned to your face. It shows in your eyes, your posture, and your mannerisms. This is possible for you, and it's what I wish for everyone. Find comfort in knowing that there is no need for you to go it alone. You can have the support you need to conquer burnout in your life.

About Dr. Veerle

Dr. Veerle Van Tricht brings a wealth of experience to individuals around the world through her work as an eye surgeon and as a Medical Mojo Mentor, specializing in helping professionals avoid burnout. Burnout is an important focus to Veerle because she has personally experienced it and it is yet to be recognized as a medical condition. As part of her own healing and recovery process, she focused on holistic solutions that would get her past the tough times and onto a strong foundation to grow from. With what she learned, she created the Burnout Resuscitation Program.

Born in a small Belgian town, Veerle always strived to make a difference in the world that extended beyond her hometown. After receiving her PhD, she went on to become an Ophthalmologist. Since that time, Veerle has worked with international organizations such as Doctors Without Borders, as well as for the public health system in Britain and South Africa. At the other scope of the spectrum, Dr. V. owned private practices in Belgium and Australia. Today, she bases her practice in the UK and has performed over 10,000 eye procedures over the years, throughout many countries.

However, the passion that Veerle has to help professionals live a balanced and fulfilling life has become a driving force for her. From her own experiences of realizing the significant challenges that existed for many professionals – especially women – with managing both a career and a personal life, she saw the underlying urgency that many people have in their life.

Today, she has taken her message to the people and is a sought out international speaker. She inspires to teach people how to rise from and manage burnout symptoms. The Burnout Resuscitation Program is a solution-oriented, lifestyle management program that is helping people find balance in their exhausted minds and bodies. According to Veerle, "Finding balance in life is essential. No one should have to choose between personal and professional fulfilment. You can have both." She is also a Reiki Master, an Angel healer certified by Doreen Virtue, PhD, an Intuitive Life Coach, and a Journey Practitioner—all which are wonderful additions to help her be a better surgeon, mentor, and healer.

Veerle is also the author of the book, *My Surgeon Talks to Angels: A Journey from Science to Faith*. This is the story that connects her personal life with her work as a surgeon, and is an inspiring account of the lives she has impacted and those that have impacted her. As a co-author with Jack Canfield in the book *Success Starts Today*, Veerle is accomplishing another goal, as she has always been inspired by the work of Jack Canfield.

Today, Veerle resides in Brampton Cumbria, UK, with her three young children. She delights in their adventures together, and enjoys living a lifestyle that celebrates all that comes with living a life of balance in all she does.

For any queries contact Dr. Veerle's website:
- www.burnoutexpert.co.uk

CHAPTER 3

SELLING KNIVES & CHANGING LIVES
A FORMULA TO CREATE MORE SYNERGY AT WORK AND AT HOME

BY DANIEL CASETTA

Our goal was to be #1. But there was a problem. 109 other teams had the same goal that Summer, and only one team could win. I was 20 years old, and the sales organization I was working with had given me an opportunity to run a summer sales office in the San Francisco Bay Area between my junior and senior years of college. This was a program that existed nationwide for top student achievers in the company, which recruited mostly college students to sell Cutco knives. That year, there were 110 of these summer offices in the company. One of these offices, in Madison, Wisconsin, opened up a wide lead midway through the 18-week competition. We were in fifth place nine weeks in, and the Wisconsin office was almost doubling our sales at that point. With the biggest sales weeks of the Summer ahead of us, we started our charge.

We closed the gap from $66,000 down to about $11,000 going into the final week of the Summer competition. With only one week left, that deficit was thought to be insurmountable. But in that final week, miracles occurred. My sales team of about three dozen mostly 18-20 year olds rallied to achieve a mutual goal that we had been talking about all Summer. Just one of the many compelling stories from that week was the rep we hadn't seen for about two months walking into the office with an order on the final night of the competition asking, "Did we win?!?" He had been in the hospital with a terrible stomach ailment that had literally threatened his life. "This is the last night!" we told him. He called his sister and got one more $28 order over the phone.

We submitted our final orders that night and then had to wait three days for the final official results to be announced. When those final numbers were posted, the Madison, WI office had sold $311,309 for the Summer. My San Mateo, CA team finished at $311,321.

We all learned a lot that Summer. We learned about teamwork, and how every single person — in this case, every single ORDER — can make the difference. We learned about leadership and inspiration, and how you can get people to care so much about mutual goals that they'd do almost anything (even literally coming from a hospital bed to the office to contribute to a sales competition) to support each other. Most importantly, we all learned some valuable lessons about creating a synergistic culture in ANY organization, group, or family.

I've personally led six other championship teams during my career with the same company, teams that topped hundreds of others during a full year in sales. I was an integral part of eleven consecutive Regional national champions. I have also developed eleven people who won their own national championships at various levels of the business. Many of my young "pupils" have gone on to create great success in their current work teams across a broad range of industries. Eventually, I became the "go-to" expert in this large national sales organization on the subject of transforming team cultures and developing people. Through this quirky sales job selling knives, I have learned how to give people the tools to change their lives. I offer these concepts to you here in this chapter.

The championship teams I have built have been special. "There was almost a physical heat that radiated from your crew," was a comment made by one of my peers. If you are a leader, what you'll find here are some practical, actionable ideas that can help you create your own version of a thriving, synergistic, special team. If you're a "leader with no title" (yet), consider what might happen for you if you exemplify these concepts in your workplace or in your personal life.

First, let's define culture as it applies to any organization or group. My view is that culture is:

The most significant ATTITUDES that permeate a team, and the CONSISTENT BEHAVIORS that result.

In other words, it's the thought patterns and belief systems that people develop, which lead to their consistent actions or behaviors. This is why the ideas here are applicable to more than just a work environment. By affecting people's belief systems, we affect their behaviors. Like a spider spinning a web, we then create a culture all around us.

In order to create a culture, we must first know what culture we want to create. To figure this out, you might think about any great team that you have been a part of, whether in sports or some other endeavor.

❖ What's the best team you've ever been a part of?
❖ What made it so great?
❖ Which elements of that team would you want to bring to your current work teams or to your family or circle of friends?
❖ What attitudes would you want to permeate your teams?
❖ What consistent behaviors would you want your team members to engage in?

Related to this, consider also:

❖ What beliefs would you want your kids to develop?
❖ How would you want them to act?

If there were five critical attitudes or thought patterns that I'd want to establish on a team, here's what they would be:

1. *Integrity to one's word*
2. *A spirit of cooperation*
3. *Work ethic*
4. *A positive focus*
5. *Consistent personal growth*

Let's dive into each of these five concepts:

1. Integrity to your word is more than just honesty. It's openness, transparency, and most importantly, doing what you say you will do.

This creates a feeling of trust within an organization or group, and trust is the foundation of all great human relationships.

2. **A spirit of cooperation** is founded upon a sincere interest in others, a desire to help others succeed, and an abundance mentality — that there's plenty of success to go around for all of us. This is an enlightened way of thinking that, when practiced by all the members of a team, adds the most value to the organization and enlarges the pie for everyone who gets a part. This attitude fosters a high level of mutual support and creates a whole new level of inspiration, motivation, and accountability on any team. It leads to greater engagement of the whole team in determining vision, direction, and team objectives, and this engagement leads to greater commitment.

3. **Work ethic** isn't about working 80 hour weeks, though sometimes that can be necessary. It's more about a willingness to do what it takes to stay on track for the mutually-determined objectives I just referenced. When everyone has ownership of the goals, they are less likely to pass the buck to someone else and more likely to step up when more is required.

4. **A positive focus** is rooted in the belief that we can determine the meaning of anything that happens in our lives. Successful people learn, over time, to choose empowering meanings for any circumstance that arises in their life or business.

   • What can I learn from this situation?
   • Where's the silver lining here?
   • What should be my next steps to get back on track?

These are all questions that a superior mind trains itself to ask during tough times. When this way of thinking becomes entrenched throughout an organization, the energy of the team becomes palpable. You can feel walking in when a team of people consistently has a positive focus. These are the teams, companies, groups, and families who consistently solve problems, quickly bounce back from adversities, and simply live life on a higher plane than others do.

5. The fifth critical attitude I listed above is a desire for **consistent personal growth.** Jim Rohn is my all-time favorite teacher of personal development, and one of my favorite of his principles is this:

> *Success is not something you pursue.*
> *It's something you attract by the person you become.*

Whatever it is that you want in your company or elsewhere in your life, you have to grow to the level that makes you capable of having that success. Related to this, Rohn also taught:

> *It is difficult to maintain that which we do not attain*
> *through our own personal development.*

We've all probably seen people luck their way into certain achievements in life. Unless these people work hard to get their growth to catch up to those achievements, they will invariably experience a personal version of a "market correction." If there's one thing I have always strived to leave with the young people who have worked in my organization, it's the importance of never stopping the learning process just because they finished the formal part of their education. I finished "16th grade" when I graduated from college, but I have passed through MANY more grades in life since then. What about you?

After identifying the attitudes or beliefs that you want to form the basis of culture on your team, it's obviously important to *engage in behaviors that model the culture you want.* "Do as I say, not as I do," does not fly in the world of leadership. Not in your home, and not in your company.

If you want your team members to have integrity to their word, this starts with the leader. Do you follow through with your commitments? A mistake I often made as a young leader was to over-commit myself, to promise more than I could deliver, or to say I would do something, but then forget. One thing I learned from Les Brown was this nugget:

> *Make commitments with care,*
> *so you can honor them with integrity.*

Be more careful with what you commit to verbally. Create a reminder system to make sure that little things don't fall through the cracks. People are watching you, and are developing an impression every day of your integrity and trustworthiness. And they will follow in what they see.

This applies at home just as much as at work. What do your kids see from you? Do you do the things you say you will do? Integrity to your word. Trust. The basis of a successful culture anywhere.

> *Children have never been very good at listening to their elders,*
> *but they have never failed to imitate them.*
> ~ James Baldwin, American author

Do you want to create a greater spirit of cooperation within your work team? How can you model this through your actions? First, take the time to get to know people in your organization personally. Nothing fosters more loyalty and cooperation than sincere interest in others. Next, be generous. Generosity towards others (with your time, resources, tools, connections, even your money), when combined with sincere interest and care, creates a strong desire for reciprocity. Others will give what they can in terms of greater cooperation and synergy with the team.

I also feel it's helpful to learn to involve others in many of the processes of leading the organization. In leading my growing organization, I frequently involve my key people in important decisions. The art of doing this is to lead with carefully designed questions that are likely to elicit ideas consistent with what you (the leader) want. "Why do you think it's important that we . . ." is a great example of a question that can engage a group of people around an important concept pre-determined by the leader.

What about modeling work ethic? How does a leader do this? Sometimes it's just about putting in the hours. Every organization has its seasons when more is required. A great leader doesn't shy away from these moments, but rather sees them as opportunities to rally the troops build others' commitment accounts.

A key part of work ethic is a sense of urgency. One of my longest-term pupils in my business once told me that this was the greatest lesson he ever learned from me — a sense of urgency, valuing every opportunity, respecting every day. I like to view every day as either a plus one or a minus one. There are no zeros. At the end of the day, I ask myself, "Did I win the day?" If so, that's a plus one. Learning to win the day just once more than your competition has a powerful accumulated effect on end results. Share this concept with others, and let them see you striving to win the day, every day. I find simple concepts like detailed weekly scheduling and daily to-do lists to be very helpful here. These are easy lessons to model and share with your team.

The concept of having a positive focus is my all-time favorite "attitude" to model for others. I have conditioned myself to quickly redirect negative thinking and find the seed of benefit in every experience. It's not always easy, but I can say that it's always worth it. And the more you do this, the more the people around you will begin to model this way of being.

Years ago, I heard a wise old man talking about this concept, and about handling the normal day-to-day experiences that many people would describe as "negative." He said there's a question he would always ask himself whenever he was confronted with any challenging experience. Here's the question:

"Am I going to die right now?"

If the answer to this question is "no," then regardless of what challenge lies in front of you, you are going to be fine in the end. So, you might as well tackle it with a positive focus and high energy.

To wrap this up, let me emphasize this: In an uncommon culture, the leader provides uncommon value. One more Jim Rohn-ism I can offer here is the idea that all of us, as great leaders, should strive to. . . *"help people with their lives, not just their jobs."* As you, the leader, is continuing to learn new things and growing yourself personally, share your lessons with the others around you. As a parent, I share life lessons with my kids about every day. Similarly, as a leader, I share the lessons that I'm learning with the people in my organization. Every meeting focuses on ways that we can grow our business, of course. But there's always a little time to also talk about how we can grow ourselves. People love this, and it builds back into the first point about conveying sincere interest in and care for your people, which builds trust, creates synergy, increases commitment and leads to all the other elements of a great culture that I have described. It's all a cycle that helps create a great team, a successful organization, or a happy family.

Just as we need more people to provide leadership in the complex organizations that dominate our world today, we also need more people to develop the cultures that will create that leadership.
~ John Kotter, What Leaders Really Do – Harvard Business Review

About Daniel

Daniel Casetta helps build a dynamic culture of synergy and growth in sales teams, mastermind groups, and among his friends and colleagues around the U.S. As a respected and trusted business leader, Dan has had a profound impact on thousands of entrepreneurs, leaders, and salespeople over the past 25 years.

Dan is well-known for helping leaders build trust and cooperation among their teams, and he facilitates interactive events with groups ranging from 10 to 1000. These events are designed to train people both professionally and personally, and to leave people feeling inspired to action.

Throughout his career with the Vector Marketing / Cutco sales organization, Dan has been a one-in-a-million achiever and a transformational leader. He became the most successful and influential field manager in the nearly 70-year history of Cutco, and his programs for leading and developing teams were integral in sparking the company's rapid growth and expansion. Eventually, Dan's company created a role for him to coach and mentor top sales reps, managers, and executives from across much of the country. He teaches skills like selling, leadership, financial well-being, and personal development to the company's top talent.

Dan graduated from Santa Clara University in the Silicon Valley. He is a regular guest speaker in business classes at universities throughout the Bay Area, and he has been welcomed into multiple organizations to share insights in areas of sales training, leadership development, and creating a culture of collaboration, growth, and success. He also hosts a mastermind group containing some of the most successful CEOs and executives in the Silicon Valley, and he participates in other such gatherings of leaders all across the country.

Personally, Dan is a husband, father of two, trusted friend to many, and gives back to his community and to others. His passion is in adding value to the world and leaving positive ripples everywhere he goes.

You can connect with Dan at:
- www.dancasetta.com
- www.facebook.com/dancasetta
- www.linkedin.com/in/dan-casetta-71b6179/

CHAPTER 4

LIVE LIKE YOU WERE DYING

BY RHONDA BARRY

It was August 27, 2002. Swallows chirped happily outside my office window as the sun streamed across my desk. But at this moment, simple pleasures almost seemed like an annoying distraction to the constant flood of chatter filling my mind. What have I done with my life? What kind of mother have I been to my children? *What legacy will I leave behind? What haven't I done yet that I really wanted to? What will I be remembered for?* The questions whirred on and on in my mind.

First one tear and then another trailed down my cheek, landing silently on the surface of my desk. It had been a long and tiring six weeks of sleepless nights tossing and turning, with large wine glasses filled to the brim, hoping for a moment of relief or distraction as the throbbing pain in my side grew stronger with each worried thought. My mind drifted back to the last appointment with my gynecologist six weeks earlier and the concern in her voice as she shared the result of the ultrasound. The ovarian cysts weren't shrinking as she'd hoped. In fact, they'd almost doubled in size. It looked like surgery was going to be an only option.

But surgery was not something that scared me. I'd always healed well and since I was self- employed, time off wasn't an issue. I actually breathed a sigh of relief that at last this issue was going to be resolved. It was her next few words that gripped me. "There's a blood test I'd like to do to see if there are cancerous cells present." Cancerous cells? *Cancer??*

First, the words screamed in my ears and reverberated there. Then they seemed to fragment and dissolve as my body went cold and my mind numb. I moved robotically as she instructed me to lie back so she could examine me, pressing here and there. "Does this hurt? What about this?" as she manipulated first the left, then the right side of the pelvic area.

Is it possible that the pain could be both intense and dull at the same time? So confusing. My mind filled with everything; then nothing. Nothing was making sense. The doctor then pressed this time on my breasts; first on the left, then on the right, then on the left again, her brow furrowed.

Her lips began to move and I heard the word 'mass', then 'large solid mass', 'surgeon' and 'biopsy'. Only fragments of the sentences registered in my mind. I felt like I was observing myself on the examining table, like the proverbial fly on the wall, disconnected from the feelings of the woman being examined on the table below.

As she quietly closed the office door behind her, I mechanically rose and dressed myself, retrieved my keys from the belly of my purse, and mechanically put one foot in front of the other, wanting to escape to the safety of my car. I don't really remember driving those first few blocks away from the clinic. Idling at a red light, a sudden strong urge gripped me. "I need to talk to mom."

As the light shifted from red to green, I clutched the steering wheel with one hand, while I fumbled with my cell phone in the other. "Please be there. Please, please, please, please."

"Hello?" Her gentle, familiar voice answered. Thank God she was there! I felt calm and safe for a brief instant until I remembered the reason for my call, and the dreaded words caught in my throat, escaping in jagged breaths. I pulled over to the side of the road, unable to see the curb as tears flooded my eyes. Mom then did what she does best. She reassured me that everything would be fine, and she would be there for anything I needed.

So, here it was, six weeks later, as I sat at my desk in my office and stared at the next day's appointments on my calendar. Tomorrow I would hear the results of both tests – the blood test and the biopsy. I'd been trying so hard to be brave (my mother labeling me a 'stoic'), pretending everything was just fine, painting on a grin whenever anyone was around.

But behind that smile the constant chatter continued in my head and the uneasy feeling in my stomach persisted. Thankfully, only one more night. I silently dreaded spending the evening at home, with the clock slowly ticking away each second.

The ringing of the phone startled me. I checked the caller ID, knowing that I would not be able to have a productive, focused call with a client. Oh good. It was Dave, my husband. I put on my happy voice, not wanting to reveal the hole of depression I'd dug for myself. He was calling to suggest that I have an evening out with the girls – perhaps a nice dinner and a relaxing glass of wine. That sounded like the perfect distraction.

A few hours later, appetite satisfied, a warm glow from the wine and great company, I unlocked the back door of the house and stood, dumfounded, in the back entryway. Five steps above me was our closed kitchen door, papered from top to bottom with bright white poster paper. My eyes darted to the drawings first. There was my company logo that meant so much to me; then one of my favorite things in the world, a decorated Christmas tree; and another favorite, shooting stars, scattered all over the paper. My focus moved on to the writing. A message from mom, one from dad, one from each of my children, my siblings, my friends and one from Dave himself. Encouraging, loving, heartfelt messages. A sob caught in my throat as I realized Dave had spent the entire evening calling family and friends for messages of support for me. And there they all were, in bright colors, an 8-foot message of love. I couldn't take my eyes off that door.

My heart began to swell, and deep inside me, something began to bubble up – the truth. I was not alone. I was dearly loved. In fact, I was surrounded by love. And I knew that whatever the results tomorrow, it would all be okay. I had all the love and support I needed to handle whatever was before me. I slept like a baby that night, wrapped in those messages of love.

I attended the appointments with renewed energy the next day. At both appointments, I received miraculous results. No abnormal cells. No cancer. I would be fine. I was going to live.

I also knew, from that moment on, my life would be different. I would begin, that very day, to create the life I wanted. To leave a powerful legacy. To BE the mother, daughter, sibling, friend I wanted to be. To live *purposefully.*

These experiences – the ovarian cysts, the solid mass in my breast, the dreaded threat of cancer, and the reminder of the incredible love and support that surrounds me – gave me three life-altering 'ah-ha' moments.

First, I was reminded: ***Life is short!*** Why do we sometimes wait for the Universe to remind us of this? It is so very easy to get caught up in the day-to-day patterns and live our lives unconsciously. Margaret Bonnano said, "It is only possible to live happily ever after on a moment-to-moment basis." Special time spent with family; a child greeting us with a leaping hug; cradling a tender newborn as they drift off into peaceful sleep; watching with pride as grown children lovingly parent their offspring; creating an 'ah-ha' moment in a classroom; assisting a client to move past a fear or achieve the results they're after; and taking the time to recognize and celebrate those around us. These are the moments that count.

During those long, worrisome months of 2002, the Universe helped me to internalize and accept the reality that yes, indeed, life IS short for all of us! Any day could bring news of an illness. Any day we could face accidents or injuries. Any day could provide a life-altering experience – for ourselves, for those we love and adore, or for those we simply pass on the street.

I've come to realize that there's incredible beauty in the message, "Life is short." For any day can also bring precious, memorable moments, like the one Dave created for me in 2002. It can bring joy, laughter and heartfelt conversations and connections with others when we take the time to really pay attention. When we take the time to listen more; to connect more; to hug more; to smile, laugh, dance and play more; and when we challenge ourselves to BE more.

I love listening to the song *Live Like You Were Dying*, released by country star Tim McGraw in 2004. What would you do differently if you knew you were dying? Would you go sky diving? Rocky Mountain climbing? Would you love deeper? Speak sweeter? Give forgiveness you've been denying?

There is great benefit in living like we are dying. Life becomes sweeter. More dynamic. More precious. More filled to the brim with glorious moments we can savour through to our last days here on earth. Harriet Beecher Stowe said, *"The bitterest tears shed over graves are for words left unsaid and deeds left undone."*

Next, I learned that *a terrible experience can be turned around when someone cares enough to create a special moment.* It was amazing how quickly my focus shifted from illness to love and support as I stood in that back entryway on that August evening, looking up at the poster paper covering the door. What an incredible gift of a magical moment. We have that power. We create our lives on a moment-to-moment basis and can determine, in any moment, what we want to create for ourselves, and others.

Medical research shows us that oxytocin (the 'feel good' chemical) is produced in our body when we think good thoughts or have pleasant experiences. When we are the recipient of an act of kindness, our oxytocin levels go up, and we feel good. When we see or hear about an act of kindness, our oxytocin levels go up. And here's the really great thing – when we DO an act of kindness, our oxytocin levels go up! We can learn to make ourselves feel good simply by pausing to remember some of the special moments others have created for us, or by creating a special moment for someone else! It's all in our hands.

Finally, I learned: *I have so much more love and support than I realized.* Often, when our lives are not working the way we want, we can feel alone in our discomfort or misery. We sometimes put on a mask of 'everything's just fine', while we suffer alone in silence. We hesitate to ask for support. We don't want to appear weak, or to bother others with our troubles. But here's the truth: Often the people in our lives want to help but don't know how they can. Or they aren't even aware there is a problem.

It's often amazing, when we take stock of how many people we have in our lives to love, and who love and support us, we discover those who always listen and support; we discover our cheerleaders; we discover those who disregard our bad habits and idiosyncrasies; we discover who we can count on.

It's been said that what we send out, we get back. I have found that to be true in my life tenfold. We have the ability to create special, memorable and even life-altering moments – for ourselves – for our family and friends – for our co-workers – and for strangers. Small actions. Random acts of kindness. Showing appreciation. Creating rituals and meaningful events. And paying it forward when we are blessed to have a moment created for us.

With kindness, we can be the veritable pebble in the pool, creating a ripple of love, a river of oxytocin to heal ourselves and the world, one moment, one kindness at a time.

So, are you ready to live like you were dying? To live intentionally? To savour life's moments? To create memorable moments for yourself and others? My experience, dear reader, is that this skill is one that is foundational to true success.

About Rhonda

Known by her clients as the Wizard of 'AH's – for her ability to put the 'AH' in training - Rhonda Barry has spent the past 35 years in the field of corporate training and development. She has designed and presented technical, motivational and skills development programs (both nationally and internationally) for management, supervisory and front-line employees and is a master in the areas of facilitation, leadership, teamwork, training simulation design, Train the Trainer and Accelerated Learning methodologies.

In addition to her proprietary programs, Rhonda is certified to deliver *Myers Briggs Type Indicator, Crucial Conversations, Crucial Accountability, Influencer – The New Science of Leading Change* and *Getting Things Done – The Art of Stress-Free Productivity.* She is an avid student of brain research, communication technologies, teaching and learning methodologies and processes for pain-free change and transition (both personal and corporate).

To enhance her effectiveness, Rhonda sought out extensive training in the use of Accelerative Learning Techniques and Therapeutic Metaphors, and became a certified practitioner of Neuro Linguistic Programming, Hypnotherapy and Time Line Therapy. Her passion is making sure every learning event she leads is filled with 'AHA' moments that significantly impact and enhance the lives of her participants. Her learning events are not only filled with fun and receive top marks, they consistently *double* industry standards for learning gain and retention.

Rhonda is also extremely passionate about creating memorable moments in her life, and for helping others do the same. She is presently putting the finishing touches on her soon to be released book, *Pretend Birthdays and Other Memorable Moments* – a treasure-trove of inspiring stories, examples and ideas for creating special moments for family and friends, at work, for strangers, and even for yourself – a book that has been endorsed by the master of memorable moments himself, Mark Victor Hansen. In 2003 Rhonda was a finalist in the YWCA Women of Distinction awards in the area of Leadership and Business – and has been profiled as an Inventive Woman in Canada for her innovative and successful training techniques.

She is a proud member of the Positive Deviant Network – a network of committed, socially-minded individuals, which includes dynamic industry leaders and teachers of The Secret, who truly celebrate positive deviance and differences – a network that intends to mid-wife humanity's transition from scarcity-based independence to abundance-based interdependence.

Rhonda is a published author, whose time is spent writing, designing learning events, facilitating corporate and personal development programs, volunteering (in the community and beyond), enjoying time with her family and creating moments that make a difference.

You can connect with Rhonda at:
- Rhonda@TheAHFactor.com
- www.facebook.com/Pretend-Birthdays-and-Other-Memorable-Moments-130352213645833/
- Twitter: @RhondaLBarry

CHAPTER 5

THE IMPACT OF ONE-ON-ONE: THE CONNECTION THAT CEMENTS YOUR SUCCESS

BY JW DICKS & NICK NANTON

It was what you might call a nice problem to have.

The rock group was experiencing such massive success in their home country that it was becoming impossible to stay directly in touch with their fans. Actually, it was becoming impossible even to play live for them, as the crowds cheered so loudly at their concerts that they couldn't even hear the music that had supposedly brought them there in the first place.

So, increasingly, there was no way for the group's members to directly communicate with the people who bought their music, the fans they depended on to keep their success afloat. Even the official fan club the management of the group had formed couldn't keep up with the demand—on average, they were three weeks behind in answering its own fan club mail, not to mention the mail coming in from the many unofficial fan clubs throughout the country.

Finally, the group's press agent had an idea. He remembered how the Queen of England always delivered her Christmas message to her subjects every year on December 25th. Why not have the group record a personal holiday message to their fans and send it out right before the holidays?

And so, in December of 1963, thousands of UK teenagers, most of them female, were excited beyond belief when they received an unexpected "flexi-disc" (a recording stamped onto a flimsy piece of plastic) in the mail. And when they put it on their phonographs to play, they were even more excited to hear four Liverpool lads singing a gibberish version of the old Christmas carol, "Good King Wenceslas," and then talking to their fans directly, utilizing the goofy humor and good-natured fun that marked the Beatles' early years of success, but also taking the time to thank them for their part in the group's ascent to legendary status.

From 1964 to 1969, John, Paul, Ringo and George continued to send out their wacky Christmas messages to their fans until the band finally disbanded. And those Christmas messages vividly illustrate what every one of you need to do to really create impact once you've established a following—and that's *communicate effectively and directly* with that following. After all, these are the people you've created a relationship with, and, as in every relationship, you have to put some work into it to make it bloom.

Why is this so important? Simple. If you tend to your following and keep them motivated by your message, they become your biggest advocates— meaning, they can win you more and more followers through their networks. As most of you already know, word-of-mouth is the most powerful form of marketing. People trust the folks they already know and like—and are more than happy to take their advice. By creating your own army of advocates, you trigger a continuous and ongoing effort that will win you more raving fans and a larger base from which to grow.

MASTERING THE ONE-ON-ONE WITH MANY

The title of this chapter may seem a little misleading. Even though we're calling it "The Impact of One-On-One," we're still talking about messaging to many. There's a simple reason for that—once you've gathered a certain number of followers, it's impossible to touch base with them individually on an ongoing basis. There just aren't enough hours in the day.

But that's just why the Beatles made it a priority to record their Christmas messages, despite their insanely hectic schedule. These days, pop stars take to YouTube, Twitter and other forms of social media to talk to their fans. They may not have the time or the ability to talk to each of their millions of fans one-on-one, but they can still successfully *simulate* the effect of reaching out to their audiences as if each person was the only one they are talking to.

And that's just the effect you're after, as if you want to become a true "MediaMaster"—our term for a thought leader who knows how to leverage both old and new media—to build the most powerful platform possible.

In the early 1960's, the Beatles had to send out records to create one-on-one communication with the many. In the 21st Century, however, there are any number of other old and new media vehicles that will allow you to reach a large audience, vehicles that still allow for this kind of one-on-one approach. The benefits of this approach are multifold—it builds loyalty and increased motivation with your base, as well as strengthens your brand over the long haul.

THE SEVEN "B'S" OF ONE-ON-ONE COMMUNICATION

Effective one-on-one communication requires certain aspects of tone and content in order to create the strongest possible connection with your audience. Following are seven of the most important elements you need to address to make that connection a real bonding experience:

1. Be Emotional

We are going to go out on a limb and boldly predict robots will never take over the world. Why? Because people only respond to those who communicate with feeling – and robots suck at that.

Yes, we're kidding and we know that if it comes down to it, the robots might have the advantage of being bulletproof. But from a persuasion standpoint, they're not mechanically equipped to demonstrate real heart...at least for now.

And that's why the flesh-and-blood politicians, public speakers and even fledging MediaMasters who actually do seem like robots have a very low ceiling to their success. If, in their media and live appearances, they can't muster any spontaneity or genuine spark, folks aren't going to respond to them. Intellectual arguments alone don't carry the day for a MediaMaster—as we all know, emotion is almost always required to make a sale.

And by the way, when we say, "Be Emotional," we're not necessarily talking about being all warm and cuddly in your messaging. There are plenty of MediaMasters who project a strong empowering persona that's filled with tough and effective bombastic flourishes. The point is, there's emotion behind those powerful personas too— and that emotion will help you connect with a significant-sized audience.

2. Be Positive (After You're Negative)

All of us are bombarded with a lot of negativity in our lives. From the daily news to our own personal struggles, we all have enough stress dumped on our heads to deal with on a regular basis. So pretty much the last thing we need is someone to add any more feel-bad moments into the equation.

That's why a MediaMaster ultimately needs to provide solutions and not just list problems. Of course, you'll want to introduce pain points to make your message resonate, but that pain has to be framed in such a way that you are seen to be someone who can alleviate it. If your messaging isn't ultimately uplifting, the public is going to have a difficult time getting on board with it.

For example, during the 2016 election, you might remember Donald Trump shouting about what a wreck America had become. But, at the same time, he positioned himself as the person to right the ship and take it in the proper direction. Whether you agreed with him or not, it was an effective political strategy that tapped into people's frustrations. And his main vehicle for his one-on-one communication? . . . Twitter, which he used to directly deliver his uncensored thoughts to the American people.

3. Be Exclusive

Everyone likes to feel like an insider. Everyone likes to feel they're part of something special that others either don't know about or are not smart enough to appreciate. Everyone likes to feel like they know something that other people don't.

With this in mind, consider yourself the president of your own club—and make all your fans feel like they're members. Create a "just-between-you-and-me" vibe that indicates they're part of an exclusive circle and are being granted wisdom that others aren't privy to.

4. Be Inclusive

Let's get back to those robots we were talking about earlier. You know, the ones who definitely *aren't* going to take over the world?

Well, here's another reason it 'ain't gonna' happen. Robots lack empathy—they can't relate to others. And people don't trust those who don't seem to understand them. So, even though our mechanical friends can solve complicated calculus problems with amazing alacrity, they don't have a shot at becoming our Supreme Rulers, because they have no idea how to talk to us.

There's no reason, however, why you, as a human being, can't avoid that fatal pitfall.

All successful MediaMasters know how to relate to their audiences and create a "we're in this together" bond. By tapping into and acknowledging their emotions—and admitting you also experience the same emotions—you create a relationship based on your shared concerns.

Use the kind of inclusive language that really drives this idea home. Phrases like "as you know," "I'm sure you agree," and "we all know" make your audience feel they're a part of your select group.

5. Be Clear

This "B" seems incredibly self-evident, but many would-be thought leaders get lost in the weeds when it comes to communicating their ideas. The old acronym, K.I.S.S.—"Keep It Simple, Stupid"—still holds to this day. Just because you're an expert on your subject does not mean your audience is, so you have to remember to keep your content and presentations grounded in the basics before you build to any lofty ideas or complex information.

6. Be Repetitive

There's a piece of wisdom that's well-known among advertising executives, which is this: Just about the time you're getting sick of a campaign, it's just beginning to register with the public. In other words, the only way to really make your message stick with people is to keep delivering it whenever you can, even though you may feel like a broken record that keeps replaying the same track over and over.

Brands become memorable not just by being consistent, but also through sheer repetition—it's the only way you can be sure that the most people not only hear your message, but also retain it.

So, while you can feel free to change up parts of your speeches and content, always make sure to return to your primary themes at some point. Reinforce, rather than reinvent; otherwise, you're throwing away all the time you've put into building your brand to this point.

7. Be Beneficial

You always want your audience to walk away feeling they've gained something—and, with all due respect to Oprah, it doesn't have to be anything near as big as a new car. It can just be a new perspective on life, a new way to grapple with a life or career issue, some useful information or just some straight up hope and inspiration. It's up to you as a MediaMaster how you deliver value. You just have to make sure that value is recognizable and memorable.

If you don't provide a benefit to your audience in some form, then, frankly, there's no compelling reason for them to become a follower. So, at least, give them a powerful takeaway with your brand—leave them with a positive message that promises transformation in their lives on some level to make the maximum impact as a MediaMaster.

MODERN METHODS OF ONE-ON-ONE COMMUNICATION

There are more options than ever before that enable MediaMasters to create the intimate impact of the one-on-one experience. We're going to detail a few of them below, including our personal favorite.

- **Podcasts**

  In 2009, an obscure middle-aged comic had hit a career dead-end. He had anger issues and a substance abuse problem that had damaged his reputation and his agent basically told him he couldn't get him any more stand-up gigs. Broke, frustrated and at the end of his rope, he went into his garage, set up a primitive recording studio and began recording a twice-a-week podcast, just to try something new.

  Six years later, President Barack Obama decided that podcast was a big enough deal that he showed up at that door of that garage, with secret service leading the way, in order to record an episode.

  Marc Maron did such an effective job of one-on-one communicating in his podcast that it attracted incredibly influential guests (besides the President, everyone from Mel Brooks to Bruce Springsteen) and suddenly, his stand-up sets began selling out. He also landed his own TV show. And all this success started with a humble podcast created in a garage.

  Podcasts give you the opportunity to directly talk to your followers and potentially grow their numbers—without censorship or commercial interruption. You're also able to bring on other experts and thought leaders that complement your message and add to your leadership positioning.

  The downside here is that there are a billion podcasts out there these days. Unless you already have a solid base of supporters, it can be hard to generate listenership. So, you need to put a killer marketing plan in place to boost the podcast's popularity. The bottom line is that it is a cheap and easy form to both create and distribute; so if you have something compelling to say, it's worth the effort.

- **YouTube**
Where can you find many of the current MediaMasters who are under 30? Or even under 20? On YouTube. There are teenagers making seven figures just from their makeup tutorial channels on that site. A couple times a week, these young DIY video superstars post content in which most of them talk directly to the camera and establish that all-important one-to-one bond. Through this technique, they build the kind of intimate relationships with their fans that keeps them hungry for more.

It's another example of how the one-on-one template keeps morphing and evolving with technology. And even though most of these YouTube superstars are geared to Millennials, there's no question that in the near future, as this generation grows older, thought leaders will be leveraging this tactic more and more to reach their following.

- **Other Social Media Sites**
Twitter, Instagram and Facebook, among other sites, are, of course, amazing places to interact with followers and create one-on-one conversations with impact. But there might also be value in participating on other social sites such as Quora.com, where users look for answers to random questions. It's the kind of place where you can demonstrate your expertise and your brand to a whole new audience that's already interested in the field you're working in. Its pool of users may not equal those of the social media giants, but it still gathers 100 million unique visitors a month.

- **Newsletters**
For our money, the newsletter is probably the most effective way to communicate with your base in a one-on-one manner. That's the reason we make sure the one we deliver to our 50k subscribers, ThoughtLeader® Magazine, is of high quality and constructed to make maximum use of the format. It also has the following regular features to both deliver value to our readers and make its proper marketing impact:

  - **A picture of us on the front page** – No, we don't do this because we're narcissists. We do this to establish a personal connection, so our clients can see who we are and key in to our personalities.

- **Columns by each of our four partners** – We want readers to hear our individual voices and also understand what each of us brings to the table at our agency. By providing value from all four of us, we can demonstrate the collective benefit of working with us.

- **A guest column by a client** – By providing a platform for our expert clients, we give them valuable exposure and also demonstrate to our subscribers the kinds of quality professionals we work with. We're also supplying our readers with other valuable content they won't get elsewhere.

- **A calendar of our agency events** – This enables people to see what we're up to, the kinds of services we provide and the unique events we're involved with (the Grammys, our own client gatherings, etc.). That, in turn, gives more scope and dimension to our agency in their eyes.

- **A welcome to (and list of) our new clients** – This not only makes our new clients feel welcomed and appreciated, it also highlights the fact that we're continually growing and continually working with new and credentialed people.

- **Offers** – Almost everything we've listed up to this point has been about providing value to our readers. However, there's also nothing wrong with selling our unique services and letting clients know what opportunities we can create for them. And note that we save most of our marketing for the very end of the newsletter, so it doesn't look like in any way, shape or form that it's just about selling. Instead, we allow genuine information and value to dominate our newsletter, so it provides a big benefit for our readership.

We love to use our newsletter for our primary mode of one-to-one communication because we can juggle a variety of information and reach many of our MediaMaster goals in one fell swoop. It's also very easy for our very busy subscribers to read it at their leisure and refer to it if they want to follow up on anything. It also doesn't take up a lot of our subscribers' time—a podcast, for example, might require a half-hour to an hour time commitment. We also, most importantly, send a physical copy of this newsletter to the mailboxes of our best clients and prospects. By changing the medium, from online to physical, it helps our content stand out from the crowd. It also shows that we value our content enough to spend the time, energy, effort and money to design it, print it and mail it—so they should value it enough to consume it!

Using one-on-one communication is an integral part of any successful MediaMaster's methodology. When your audience feels you're talking to them as individuals and successfully reflecting their emotional wants and needs, they're going to respond with passion and enthusiasm. And that can't help but catapult you to higher and higher levels of success!

About JW

JW Dicks, Esq., is a Wall Street Journal Best-Selling Author®, Emmy Award-Winning Producer, publisher, board member, and co-founder of organizations such as The National Academy of Best-Selling Authors® and The National Association of Experts, Writers and Speakers®.

JW is the CEO of DNAgency and is a strategic business development consultant to both domestic and international clients. He has been quoted on business and financial topics in national media such as *USA Today, The Wall Street Journal, Newsweek, Forbes, CNBC.com,* and *Fortune Magazine Small Business.*

Considered a thought leader and curator of information, JW has more than forty-three published business and legal books to his credit and has co-authored with legends like Jack Canfield, Brian Tracy, Tom Hopkins, Dr. Nido Qubein, Dr. Ivan Misner, Dan Kennedy, and Mari Smith. He is the Editor and Publisher of *ThoughtLeader®* Magazine.

JW is called the "Expert to the Experts" and has appeared on business television shows airing on ABC, NBC, CBS, and FOX affiliates around the country and co-produces and syndicates a line of franchised business television shows such as *Success Today, Wall Street Today, Hollywood Live,* and *Profiles of Success.* He has received an Emmy® Award as Executive Producer of the film, *Mi Casa Hogar.*

JW and his wife of forty-three years, Linda, have two daughters, three granddaughters, and two Yorkies. He is a sixth-generation Floridian and splits his time between his home in Orlando and his beach house on Florida's west coast.

About Nick

An Emmy Award-Winning Director and Producer, Nick Nanton,Esq., produces media and branded content for top thought leaders and media personalities around the world. Recognized as a leading expert on branding and storytelling, Nick has authored more than two dozen Best-Selling books (including *The Wall Street Journal* Best-Seller, *StorySelling™*) and produced and directed more than 40 documentaries, earning 5 Emmy Awards and 14 nominations. Nick speaks to audiences internationally on the topics of branding, entertainment, media, business and storytelling at major universities and events.

As the CEO of DNA Media, Nick oversees a portfolio of companies including: The Dicks + Nanton Agency (an international agency with more than 3000 clients in 36 countries), Dicks + Nanton Productions, Ambitious.com, CelebrityPress, DNA Films®, DNA Pulse, and DNA Capital Ventures. Nick is an award-winning director, producer and songwriter who has worked on everything from large-scale events to television shows with the likes of Steve Forbes, Ivanka Trump, Sir Richard Branson, Rudy Ruettiger (inspiration for the Hollywood blockbuster, *RUDY*), Jack Canfield (*The Secret*, creator of the *Chicken Soup for the Soul* Series), Brian Tracy, Michael E. Gerber, Tom Hopkins, Dan Kennedy and many more.

Nick has been seen in *USA Today, The Wall Street Journal, Newsweek, BusinessWeek, Inc. Magazine, The New York Times, Entrepreneur® Magazine, Forbes,* and *FastCompany.* He has appeared on ABC, NBC, CBS, and FOX television affiliates across the country as well as on CNN, FOX News, CNBC, and MSNBC from coast to coast.

Nick is a member of the Florida Bar, a voting member of The National Academy of Recording Arts & Sciences (Home to the GRAMMYs), a member of The National Academy of Television Arts & Sciences (Home to the EMMYs), Co-founder of The National Academy of Best-Selling Authors®, and serves on the Innovation Board of the XPRIZE Foundation, a non-profit organization dedicated to bringing about "radical breakthroughs for the benefit of humanity" through incentivized competition – best known for its Ansari XPRIZE which incentivized the first private space flight and was the catalyst for Richard Branson's Virgin Galactic.

Nick also enjoys serving as an Elder at Orangewood Church, working with Young Life, Downtown Credo Orlando, Entrepreneurs International and rooting for the Florida Gators with his wife Kristina and their three children, Brock, Bowen and Addison.

Learn more at:
- www.NickNanton.com
- www.CelebrityBrandingAgency.com

CHAPTER 6

DEFY THE ODDS

BY ALTHERESA GOODE HOWARD

One day, I heard that the bumble bee with the way its body is shaped and its small wings, aerodynamically, should not be able to fly. And for every butterfly we see, hundreds and thousands more didn't survive the many predators and stages that the caterpillar has to go through in order to transform into the beautiful butterfly. I thought, "the bumble bee is not supposed to be able to fly, yet it "Defies the Odds" and flies anyway. And if the caterpillar "Defies the Odds" and transforms into the beautiful butterfly, then on the things that you and I were not supposed to be able to do, we can "Defy the Odds" and do them.

So, what are your current dreams and goals? What is it that you have in your heart to do, be, achieve, accomplish or do more of? Along the way, like most of us, you may have heard how hard, challenging and difficult it will be. You may hear about others who attempted something similar, but didn't succeed.

Like Fred Smith, founder of Federal Express, you may even be told it is impossible to do what you desire to do. But guess what, some of the most successful people I know and have studied, and probably everyone who has achieved success in any field, like Oprah, Jeff Bezos of Amazon. com, Walt Disney, Les Brown and others, they were told some of those things, but they decided to "Defy the Odds" and do it anyway. So can you!

Let me share some of my story and things I and other successful people have learned and applied to encourage you to "DEFY the Odds" and achieve your goals, live your dreams and become the success you desire to be.

When I started in radio, women were primarily placed only as a midday personality or sidekick to the lead male jocks. Very few women had their own morning show or got the contracts and good salaries.

But, over the next few years, as I applied these keys, I began to be noticed and recognized. My voice began to stand out as being unique, distinctive and versatile. I became one of the few African American Women in my area to be offered a contract and given my own morning show. Now, I have enjoyed a successful career in the Radio and Music Industry for 33 years. I have authored several books (including How Bad Do You Want To Be Blessed?). I've traveled and worked with legendary motivational speaker, Les Brown. And now, I'm working with the great Jack Canfield.

But, as a child, I was insecure. My parents were divorced when I was eight years old, because my dad drank too much and became combative. Fights broke out every weekend. I developed a nervous condition and would break out in hives. I later developed severe eczema, migraine headaches and at the age of twelve, I was molested.

Yet, instead of being another statistic, following in the pattern of my dad, becoming an alcoholic, or spiraling downward into drugs and other destructive behavior, I defied the odds. I started going to church, developed a relationship with God and began to reach out to encourage others. Even before I ever achieved any success, I believed I could and I would. I believed others could as well.

Looking back over my life, encouraging and empowering people so that they will tap into their potential and walk in their greatness, is what I am passionate about; it is what I believe I am called to do. So, I say to you today, that if I can "Defy the Odds," and make it, so can you.

Now, I will agree that going after your dreams and goals may not be easy, but it's possible. So, here are a few keys that I, and countless other successful people, have utilized to reach their goals and live their dreams.

To "Defy the Odds" and succeed:

1. You must believe that "It's Possible."

When all of these devastating things were happening in my life, I could have gotten stuck in hurt, pain, hopelessness and despair, because I didn't know what the future had in store for me. But, I believed that better was possible for me. So, you have to believe that better is possible for you also. Believe that you can follow your dreams. Believe that you, too, can become successful.

2. Be clear on what you want

In the movie, Space Jams, starring basketball great, Michael Jordan, the scene starts with a young Michael outside in his backyard bouncing and shooting the basketball. His dad comes outside and sees Michael shooting the ball and making the shots. Young Michael already has thoughts of what he wants to do when he gets older, so he asks his father, "Do you think I can play (college) ball at UNC?" His dad tells him that's a fine school and he thinks it's possible. Then Michael says, (after playing college ball), he wants to go to the NBA. His father lets him know "It's possible." And then young Michael says, "and after I do all of that, then I'm going to go play Major League Baseball." And at that point, his dad tells him to slow down. It's time to go inside.

Now, in the movie, during the dialogue between Michael and his dad, there are photo clips and footage of Michael playing ball in college at UNC, playing in the NBA and then playing Major League Baseball.

That scene shows us what it looks like to have a clear goal and believe. But, though we now know Michael Jordan as the great basketball player, he didn't start that way. The first time he tried out for the basketball team in High School, he was cut. So, what did he do, quit? No!

3. Be Determined and Diligent

Michael knew he wanted to play basketball. So, he became Determined and Diligent and did what he needed to do, in order to accomplish his goals.

4. Put forth the Effort

Michael started putting forth the necessary effort to improve. He spent hours practicing, working on his ball handling and shooting. The next year, he makes the team; and the rest, as they say, is history. It is said, that even at the top of his game while in the NBA, Michael still spent hours on the basketball court working and shooting the ball from every angle on the court.

So, have clear goals (know what you want to do, be or accomplish), and be determined and diligent to learn and do what you need to do in order to achieve it. Put in the time and the effort. And next: Focus and ReFocus.

5. Focus

I have found that the most successful are people who focus on the goal, project, assignment and whatever they are wanting to accomplish. Sylvester Stallone is an actor, writer and director of the movie, ROCKY – parts 1- 6. The movie exemplifies these points and follows the story of a guy who has been boxing for a while, but has to "Defy the Odds," in order to succeed.

Rocky and his trainer know that he has what it takes to make it, but he just hasn't gotten the break. But, finally, the day comes when he gets the opportunity to fight the heavyweight champion of the world. He has a clear goal. He believes he can do it. He's determined. He's diligent. He puts forth the effort. He trains harder than he had ever trained up to that point. He is focused. And it pays off. He wins!

But then, after he becomes the champion. He enjoys his new fame, money, advantages and all the perks that can go along with success. It's interesting that successful athletes have sometimes expressed, that after being on top and then lose, it's normally because they lost their edge. They lost sight of the thing that provokes and compels them to focus. My mentor and friend, legendary motivational speaker, Les Brown, calls it 'being hungry.' He says, "You've got to be hungry."

6. You've got to be hungry

When you are not hungry, you may do just enough to get by, but when you are hungry, you do whatever it takes.

Rocky was finally successful, but became distracted by the things success can bring with it. His trainer told him he wasn't focused and training like he should for the upcoming fight. He told Rocky, "This guy is hungry, you ain't been hungry since you won the title." But Rocky didn't take it seriously. On the other hand, Clubber, the opponent, was hungry to win. He was defeated and lost his title. Clubber won.

So, in Rocky 3, Apollo Creed starts working with Rocky to help him train to regain his title. Rocky is still grieving. He lost his trainer, his title, his confidence, his focus and his champion mindset. Rocky began doubting if he could make the comeback.

It's important to surround yourself with people who can help you, encourage you, advise you and even stretch you.

During Rocky's moments of doubt and questioning his abilities, thankfully, those around him were able to encourage and remind him that he could do it.

When Rocky wasn't putting forth his best efforts, wasn't hungry to win his title back, Apollo gets upset with him and tries to provoke him into doing what he needs to do by saying, "Come on man, you got to have the eye of the tiger." That's what I think of when I say, "DEFY". "Be Determined and Diligent, put forth the necessary Effort, be Focused and surround Yourself with key people and Yield the results.

After the conversation with Apollo and then with his wife Adrian, Rocky gets refocused. He once again has a clear goal, he is determined and diligent in his training to win, he puts forth the effort, and then he yields the results. Rocky wins the title again. The thing that holds it all together and makes it work is the Champion's Mindset.

7. Develop A Champion's Mindset

You can call it a Winner's Mindset or a Success Mindset. We saw it with Michael Jordan. We saw it with Rocky and you will see it with most successful people.

A Champion with a Success Mindset understands that there may be some challenges, distractions, delays, obstacles, and setbacks. But, they don't allow those things to stop them nor cause them to give up.

It is said, that while working on the invention of the light bulb, Thomas Edison failed 10,000 times before he got it right. But, when Thomas Edison was asked about it, he didn't see it as failure. He commented that he just found 10,000 ways that didn't work, but it helped him eventually find the right way that did work.

Remember, one's own thoughts and how you see things determine what you do, what you get, how or whether or not you reach your goals or destination. If you see things as hard, then it will be hard for you. If you see a thing to be possible, then success will be within your reach. So, see success as a process. The more you learn and consistently put these keys to work, you will unlock and open up more doors and opportunities for success.

8. Be Adjustable

Being adjustable is like a secret weapon that can help you come out on top, despite what you face in life.

In Rocky 2, Apollo and Rocky trained hard for a rematch with each other. Rocky's trainer told him, in order for him to beat Apollo, he had to change the way he was used to training and fighting. Rocky was a southpaw, (left handed), so his trainer told him in order for him to gain an advantage, he had to learn how to fight right handed. Rocky said, "I can't." His trainer replied to him, "There is no can't." It was challenging to do at first, but Rocky changed and adjusted and won the fight.

In the world we live in today, things are changing so rapidly and the more we are able to adjust to the changes and know what to do and how to do it, the better off we will be.

So, despite the circumstances you may have grown up in, the environment, opposition, adversity or the things you may face in the days ahead, remember, there is a Champion in you. Success is within your reach, so GO FOR IT! And the next time you see or think about the bumble bee and butterfly flying around, be reminded of your ability to "Defy the Odds" and make it.

Much Success to You!
Altheresa

About Altheresa

Altheresa is a captivating speaker with a unique, distinct and powerful voice. She has enjoyed a successful career in the Radio and Music Industry for 30 plus years. In addition to being on Radio and TV, she does voiceover work and reads for audiobooks.

She was recently named a 2017 "Woman of Excellence" by *TV One, Urban One and Radio One* and she will receive her Doctorate Degree in May 2018.

Altheresa has traveled and worked with legendary motivational speaker, Les Brown, who calls her the speaking singer because of her diversity and her unique presentations where she inspires the audience with her message and singing.

She has authored several books, including *How Bad Do You Want To Be Blessed? How to Pray Effectively,* and D*efy The Odds - Fly, Win!* – which is scheduled to be released in June 2018.

She has worked with numerous singers, professionals, preachers, and athletes. She serves as a coach, adviser, trainer and support for leaders in Business, Music and Churches. And she is a Leader to Leaders, Pastors and Churches. She works diligently within her church and community to positively impact the lives of youth. She is also a member of Rotary and recently ran for Mayor.

She has been married for 31 years to Bishop Eddie Howard. They have three biological children, (son) Elishua, (daughters) Courtney and Aiesha, four adopted adult children and sixteen grandchildren, the youngest of which are Princess Zamari and Prince Davion, and three great grands, Princesses Syraiah and Skylar, and Prince Kaden. She also has a multitude of spiritual children and grandchildren.

"As I look at my life," she says, "I have truly been blessed. I'm living my dreams. Empowering and encouraging people to tap into their potential and walk in their greatness, is more than something that I am passionate about, it is what I believe I am called to do. So, I say to you today, that if I can 'Defy the Odds' and make it, so can you."

Altheresa's YouTube channel is AGH Empowers. She can be reached on:
- Facebook: Altheresa Goode Howard,
- Instagram and Twitter: @Altheresag

CHAPTER 7

THE 5A'S OF ACHIEVEMENT: AWARENESS, ACCEPTANCE, ATTITUDE, APPRECIATION AND AMUSEMENT

BY CATHERINE ALLON

Just after the breakout of the Hungarian Revolution, Russian tanks rolled into Budapest, Hungary, and I, along with other children in our building, stood in our lobby with our noses against the window wondering... did this mean war?

Well, my parents were not going to stay around to find out. They had barely escaped death in the Second World War. And besides, they had already lost faith in communism! There was as much addiction, poor health, disenfranchisement and poverty as ever. They discovered that communism was hierarchical, lacking justice and equality, with greed and control predominating among those in power.

People did not feel free in Hungary where their education, training, jobs, as well as where they lived were selected for them. Can you imagine? If you had an extra room they would put a stranger there; so we had filled our tiny spare bedroom with a nanny, since my parents worked till 7 pm! She earned room and board without salary, since that was all they could afford.

My parents, my brother and I, finally did escape on our second attempt with the help of a guide sent by an American family friend. We stayed with distant relatives in Austria until we could get safe passage to North America. We were headed for the U.S. but they had closed their borders to refugees from Hungary. Almost a year later, sponsored by my uncle, we landed in Montreal, Canada.

The life of an immigrant is an arduous journey. There are no easy routes to learning a new language, finding a new job, and making enough to live on. Thus, my parents placed my brother and I in a poor children's home, an orphanage really, so that they could work 12 hours a day, 6 days a week serving in the hospitality industry as busboy and waitress, and earn enough to support us. Within a year, my parents could afford a small apartment and were able to bring us home!

In the meantime, my brother and I had learned not only how to speak English, but also about living with people whose way of life was very different than ours had been in Budapest. We had to adapt to our environment or suffer the hardships of fear, loneliness and alienation. Quite innocently, I realized early on that, if I remained optimistic about eventually returning to my parents' care, I felt better, even though there was a lot to overcome before that happened!

It meant that I had to accept my situation, maintain a positive attitude with all those around me, and appreciate all that I was receiving in my unfamiliar environment. Staying aware and having a sense of humor helped me overlook some mean-spirited faces, endure the strange food, and overcome not being able to express myself in English.

At a young age, I learned the hardships of leaving my country because of war. It was difficult being without my parents, and when children did not get along because they did not accept each other's differences at the orphanage. In sharp contrast, I noticed that when I smiled and appreciated others, they treated me fairly; and at dinner, instead of leaving the turnip on my plate, I finished it and was able to have my dessert too! And when I went to sleep at night, instead of disturbing others with my crying, I made myself think of what I was grateful for. The list was not long but it did include having my bed close to the bathroom and being able to see the sun shine into the dormitory in the morning. I also enjoyed the singing and the desserts!

Through the years, I discovered that acceptance arises from facing and allowing what is, and grows through positive reinforcement. Without acceptance, there is no growth. With it begins personal transformation, peace within, and the development of healthy relationships. Have you noticed how it feels when you finally accept your parents as they are, and realize that no matter how they treated you, it was their particular brand of loving? They never intended to harm you. They thought they were doing their best with the options they had.

They too may not have been parented well by their own parents. Often parents have had to work hard to make a living, and may not have been at home much to give children all the compassion and guidance they need. Dysfunctional families have been more the rule rather than the exception, unfortunately!

What can we expect from family members, friends and others? Is it fair to ask someone to meet our needs when they are unable to meet their own, let alone fulfill them? Often it is easier to love ourselves and others, and then everything we receive is icing on the cake! We are here to improve on the way things have been. We are the 'way-showers'. It is up to us to demonstrate our willingness to be more loving, caring, kind and compassionate. This will bring untold benefits not only in how we feel, but also in our relationships with others.

Scientists have shown how trends in behavior take hold of a population and spread like wildfire when a certain number of people subscribe to a new behavior. Remember how television became popular in the 1960s and eventually, many of us were watching TV – endlessly? And still do! Unfortunately, many families have replaced more natural activities such as walking in nature, playing outside or sharing conversation at meal times – with the TV. More recently, we have all seen the growth in popularity of the cell phone within the last ten years or more! At last count, over six billion people on our planet, or almost 85%, have used a cell phone!

This is a powerful statistic to imagine! But it is a huge indicator for us all to notice that it is possible to spread great ideas! These ideas can make our world more harmonious by letting go of our negative thoughts, becoming more aware by living in the present moment and feeling peace within. Then, as we begin to feel that happiness within ourselves, it gives us energy to be more giving, productive and appreciative. It allows us to be more of who we really are.

Fast forward thirty years after the orphanage, as a psychotherapist, yoga teacher and an awareness coach, I delivered a workshop to a community college where students needed guidance and some acknowledgement of their talents. They lacked self-esteem to foster their contributions in the world. Success had brought them to a certain point but many did not appreciate it; nor did they realize how their level of awareness impacted their lives. Here was an opportunity to improve young peoples' negative attitudes and for them to realize and appreciate that they were in a program at a community college because of their own talents and dedication. Here are a few highlights from that session:

To start, I asked if anyone in the class could describe what constitutes a good attitude?

A young woman called Nora spoke up, "My mother has a good attitude. She often does the things that make her happy, supports the needy, and is able to let go of her irritations as they come up." Smiling, I acknowledged her, "That's a reliable description of how people with a sensible attitude behave. I bet she is also in pretty good health, is well-liked among family and friends and enjoys her work." Nora nodded, "Yes, so true".

I continued, "A poor attitude alone can account for a lack of success and miscommunications. It can result in anger or sadness that creates unwanted situations, ill health and suffering. However, fortunately, the quality of our attitudes is a choice and fully in our hands. We are responsible for making ourselves happy, not miserable. Happiness comes from within. Those who are not aware of their negative thoughts and feelings, or choose to deny them, may have unhappy attitudes, become victims and create unwanted tension and unnecessary hardships.

I then asked Nora and the rest of the class to pick a partner, and jot down two recent challenges and how they successfully overcame them using factual descriptions rather than judgments. I added, "Then take turns describing to your partner how you can appreciate and build on your experiences by learning from your challenges and using them as opportunities. Jot these down so you can save them for later when you're not at your best."

Later on, I asked, "How does acceptance open the door to change?"

No hands went up. I asked everyone to close their eyes and think of the worst thing they have done in their lives, and as difficult as it may be, allow themselves to accept it, even if it's for this moment only. I gave them a few minutes to ponder this idea, then feel and experience accepting the mistake. Then I asked, "How do you feel now that you have accepted yourself for the absolute worst thing that you have ever done?"

- "Lighter."
- "Free."
- "Peaceful."
- "Happy."

. . . were some of the responses.

"Do you think these feelings of being lighter, free, peaceful and happy could allow you to treat yourself and others better - perhaps even forgive others for what they have done to you?" I smiled.

"Now, I'd like you to take a few minutes each and explain to your partner how your lives would improve as a result of having more energy and fun in your life." Not surprisingly, when I called "time" at the end of ten minutes, they had not finished sharing. They asked for more time. However, the period was almost over.

So, I ended with: "When we are drained energetically, it is difficult to enjoy life and feel harmonious. Research has shown how the body needs a certain amount of energy to thrive and stay aware. Sometimes called chi or prana in the East, life force energy must be continuously replenished to engage successfully in our daily tasks. Without adequate energy, people develop addictions, such as coffee and alcohol, and the body begins to breakdown. Our immune systems weaken and can cause us to become ill. Thus, we must regain and monitor our energy levels to maintain good health.

"Notice what activities build your energy (e.g., fresh air, exercise, laughter, doing what you love, rest, good company, nurturing food, gardening, sleep). Choosing what works for you and what gives you energy could lead to more peace and happiness! Commitment and consistency are key!

"At home tonight, write down a few things that drain your energy levels (e.g., feeling sad, arguing, texting, fear, alcohol, judging, criticizing, too little sleep and overeating). Any energizing activity, even sleep, if done to excess can drain your energy. A healthy body requires a unique program for each individual and your needs and wants. Create a program for you by optimizing your energy gains and minimizing your energy drains. Moderation, not perfection, is the key! You don't have to suffer to be healthy, just stay aware of your energy level and have fun!"

Using acceptance and gratitude at the beginning or end of each day is an opportunity to build your happiness within! We could all say, "Thank you for this day, thank you for my health, thank you for my relationships, my warm home, a productive day with many challenges." ... and so on. Not only would a routine of giving thanks begin and end each day joyfully, it could create and build better relationships and even better health. What do you have to be grateful for?

Most of all, I am grateful to have the opportunity to bring you these messages so that they may open some doors for you to walk through in your lives that will make this world happier and more peaceful! Each day, I connect with people who are overcoming their challenges in life and are ready to engage in dialogues to heighten their awareness, so that together we can raise the Earth's vibrational energies and build a better future for our children and grandchildren!

About Catherine

Catherine Allon, BSc., M.Ed., has been a Spiritual Counsellor and Consultant for over twenty years. During 1990-1998, she worked as a Project Consultant at the Ontario Ministry of Health with community groups and government-funded agencies promoting health and preventing alcohol and drug addiction. In her last four years there, she served as a consultant to over 45 mental health and addiction treatment agencies, travelling all over the province and trouble-shooting with CEOs for successful program delivery and long-term staffing.

In 1998, while in Los Angeles, California, her life changed dramatically as she was awakened through a bodhisattva training called the Radical Awakening process. She walked out of that session into the light of day with her senses heightened, her mind still, and felt as though she was connected with nature and all around her. Returning to Toronto, she decided to leave her well-paid and much-loved position to help bring more awareness to the world. She had learned that she could make the greatest impact in her lifetime by bringing others her gift of awakening.

As a spiritual counsellor, her goal is to work with people who feel depressed, stuck and trapped in their lives. When people become more consciously aware, they are able to follow their passion and live a life of greater success, fulfillment and happiness.

As a Certified Kundalini Yoga Teacher since 2000, she has been teaching yoga classes in recreation and community centres, YMCAs, and privately with individuals. Kundalini Yoga is one of five ancient yogas. It is considered to be the jet version of yoga, bringing greater results more quickly. She is a Certified Laughter Yoga teacher and believes that without humor there is not enough joy, and without service and volunteering we forget to love one another.

In her volunteer capacity, she was a founding member of World Peace Associates in the 1990s, a peace organisation creating Peace Festivals in Toronto, ON, Canada, and a Roots of Empathy instructor in elementary schools in the early 2000s. Today she is the National Coordinator in Canada for The Love Foundation, a world-wide non-profit organization based in the US.

As a consultant, three of her most valued works have been her *Seven Principles for Creative Living, How to Turn Stress into Energy,* and *Active Parenting.* Her little ebook called *Connecting with the Present Moment* is available on her website.

You may connect with her at any of the following:
- Website: www.energyawakening.com
- Tel. (416) 694-0232
- e-mail: ccawaken@ca.inter.net
- Facebook/CatherineAllon
- Twitter/CatherineAllon

CHAPTER 8

THE STOCK MARKET: WHAT EVERY BEGINNER NEEDS TO KNOW

BY KRYSTLE HALL

On average, only 25% of Americans will have the necessary amount of money to retire in their current lifestyle.

Prepare for retirement. Most of us have heard these words from the minute we enter the fulltime workforce. Some listen, and others do not. After all, when you are young you feel like you have a plethora of time at your disposal. Then life happens and time flies by. Retirement is there before you know it and that's when it's too late to realize that you didn't do well enough with your investing to retire in your current lifestyle. Or sadly, you had a health issue and were forced to retire early—a double stress. And how about this scenario: you have to move in with your children or rely on them to help you out. It's the opposite of what most of us have heard in today's news, which is that Millennials are the ones who have to live at home with their parents because they cannot afford to live independently.

Being intentional in how you plan for retirement is necessary, and it's never a wise idea to think that it's either "too late" or "too early" to begin to work a plan.

The number one way that most people will build up their retirement plan is through the stock market. This is part of the reason why I developed a real passion for the stock market in college. Anything to do with stocks – websites, books, forums, classes, newspapers – I was interested in reading or participating in. Learning how the big leaders in the industry viewed stocks and exploring why certain companies outperformed others was absolutely riveting to me. It compelled me to learn for myself how to evaluate a market through my own investigative lens, not just taking the advice of others. Today, this is the inspiration and platform of my business, Stock Market Investing for Beginners (www.stockmarketinvestingbeginner.com).

It was after college, while working as a chemical engineer, that I really put the connection together between workers, retirement planning, and the real story of many Baby Boomers. They were worried about having enough money to retire, and not being able to experience life after retirement. Wondering if they'd be able to finally travel, spend time with their grandchildren, and pursue their favorite hobbies was what they were concerned about. Then it dawned on me that stocks were a potential source of income that lead to more things than retirement day, alone.

ADDITIONAL INCOME HELPS TO BUILD DREAMS

Because of this, I put all the information I learned into practice through my own 401(k) at work and began to grow it. What has unfolded is nothing short of incredible…and fulfilling.

THREE AREAS TO EVALUATE WHEN LOOKING FOR A BROKER

Not all stock brokers conduct their business the same way. You have to understand what to look for in order to evaluate the entire picture, not just a piece of it.

I'm very methodical when it comes to my research and I explore what my best choices are, especially when those choices involve my finances. Now people take advantage of that information and when they ask me about what to even look for when shopping for a broker, I tell them to focus on three areas—features, commission fees, and the quality of customer service.

1. Features

Customer service is king, even for the financial industry. This means offering ways to educate and inform their clients so they become smarter along the way. What I've always been drawn to are tutorials on their websites, videos, newsletters, and trading platform capabilities. It's a positive experience to conduct virtual trades and see how your results turned out. At a minimum, it's certainly much better than losing your real money by making bad choices. Ultimately, even though you may have a broker, you should have a sound basic understanding of how your money is being invested in the market.

2. Commission Fees

Every time you purchase or sell a stock there is a fee associated with it. If you do not pay attention to what the fees are, you could be losing money unnecessarily. The lowest trading fee isn't necessarily the best service, nor is the highest trading fee always the worst choice. You have to look at what all you are getting for that fee, including the features and quality of customer service.

3. Quality of Customer Service

In general, customer service expectations should be the same when you are paying an organization to be of assistance to you in some way. For brokers, you should expect that they call you back within a reasonable amount of time and offer explanation when necessary. Plus, you want to personally mesh with them so you have a good rapport. The last thing you need is to wonder if you're really handing over your hard-earned money to someone who isn't properly qualified. These people cannot control the market, per say, but they are a pivotal part of your investing if you choose to have them make investment decisions for you.

There are a significant number of people that fear the stock market. They've heard the horror stories and don't understand how their own outcome can be different than someone else's by just understanding a few basic concepts like what's been listed out above. Helping all people through bringing awareness to all aspects of the stock market in a non-intimidating way is the outreach that I'm doing. It feels great to help someone go from feeling scared and uncertain about the stock market to gaining the confidence to know that they can create the right dynamics to have a positive experience within it, no matter how volatile the market may be.

FUNDAMENTALS OF A GREAT STOCK

Through the methodologies of fundamental analysis and technical analysis, people can better evaluate a great stock from a struggling one.

With a combination of fundamental analysis and technical analysis, you can become successful in the stock market. Each type of analysis gives you a broad overview that leads to stronger insights. Sometimes what looks good isn't necessarily great and this is important to remember.

Fundamental Analysis
With this analysis of a particular stock you will look at the financial background of it. Key factors to look for include company revenue, earnings, return on equity, and overall consistency in the financial statement.

Technical Analysis
In technical analysis you will look at the trend movement of a company stock in regards to buying and selling. Key factors to look for are volume of shares, new highs in price, and the moving average.

Sound fundamental analysis and technical analysis are a part of the six rules listed below, which will help you learn to research and select the best stocks out there.

1. **Listed on the S&P 500 Index**

   Because we depend on the S&P 500 to better understand how the economy is doing, stock market experts tend to use this as a starting point. The companies on this list have already been assessed and are operating at a certain level. They will show evidence of great revenues, profits, corporate structure, etc. For a beginner, this takes a lot of the stress out of the evaluation.

2. **Companies with annual revenues of at least $1 billion or more**

   Mostly every company on the S&P 500 is going to meet this. The reason that it's a great metric for a good stock though is because it's a safe marker. It is very hard to go from a billion to zero quickly. You don't want to invest in the companies that can go bankrupt overnight and without notice. Having this buffer can offer you peace-of-mind.

3. Annual earnings growth rate of 20% or more is highly desirable

This has proven itself to be a wise criterion to not veer away from. A growth rate of this magnitude ties in all the aspects of what a great company should be. Excellent management, exciting products, and significant earnings can boost the growth of a company to extraordinary highs. All my research and results have shown that a minimum of 20% is acceptable. This rate should be consistent from year to year...and of course, the higher the better.

4. Average trading volume of one million shares or more shows liquidity

This is important to evaluate because an average trading volume of at least one million shows solidity. It shows that people are actively trading the stock, which demonstrates that they are heavily invested in the potential of the company's future. Liquidity indicates a company that might not be going bankrupt the next day or week so the million share marker shows promise.

5. New price highs for the stock (Current price near the high of the 52-week range)

By looking at the historical data and the past year to see the current prices for comparison you can see if a stock is high, low, or where it's expected to be. An "underperforming" stock will show that it's not growing as quickly as it should be. Why? That's often the unknown, but it could be internal issues with management, quality assurance, or any other number of variables. Make sure you investigate further into any stocks you want and find out the full story. At a minimum, consider this a caution flag before you proceed.

6. Exciting, new company products and press releases

I have found Yahoo Finance to be an invaluable source for reading press releases from companies as to what they have on the horizon— if there is anything that may grow the company further or stall it.

Whether it's good or bad, it's smart to learn about. Bad press releases should lead to reconsideration of a stock.

FIVE COMMON MISTAKES THAT INVESTORS MAKE

*A few basic insights can help you to avoid a mistake
that leads to a big financial loss.*

Understanding the stock market and using it to grow your finances and see the exciting benefits it offers is meant to be a positive, fruitful experience. And it can be if you avoid some of the more common mistakes many investors – both new and experienced – have made.

1. Listening to rumors and TV analysts telling you what to buy

I avoid rumors at all costs. Keep it simple and only rely on factual information to make your investment decisions. I actually enjoy watching TV analysts so I can listen to their opinions on why that's the stock to watch. Once in a while they may mention a great stock that wasn't previously on my radar. When this happens I conduct my own research to see whether it's worth me investing in. It occurs about 10% of the time, which isn't very high.

2. Holding losing stocks while hoping they eventually go back up

Hoping that a stock will magically go back up is not a good plan. You will only be very disappointed if you do not sell the stock immediately to prevent a significant loss. A common mistake is to buy stocks while it's averaging down instead of going up. This means that as the stock continues to trickle down, people continue to buy more of the stock since they see it as a bargain. Unfortunately, in most cases the stock is heading towards zero and does not bounce back up again. It is profitable to buy more of the stock while it is heading in an upward trend. The trick is to learn how to determine the exact moment to buy before the stock takes a rapid increase.

3. Not following the rules and buying a stock based on your emotions

Guessing is not a method. This is not the same as gambling in a casino where there is only a small chance you can win. Having the right mindset in stock trading will reduce the potential of many avoidable errors. Stay focused on your long-term goals to continue on the path towards greatness. When you follow the six rules mentioned earlier for spotting a good stock, you increase your chances of success. This is important for many reasons, not the least of which is retirement.

4. Buying too much all at once instead of starting out in small steps

It may be tempting to buy a bit of everything if it seems good, but start out slow so you don't lose any significant amounts of money. When you are learning you want to take calculated risks and see how they pan out. Once you have completed all the research on your chosen stock, start with only one or two companies to learn how the stocks move in the chart. As time goes on, you'll recognize winning patterns and be able to be more aggressive with your portfolio.

5. Not learning from your trading mistakes so you can keep improving

The only way you can improve on something is if you learn from your mistakes. This is how you grow smarter and learn lessons. After each trade, write down what went well or wrong to figure out the "why". In some cases, you may have to try different methods or conduct better research on your stocks to get better at investing. My website does list out some of the ways to do this more than this basic information.

IT'S NEVER "TOO LATE" TO START

Save today and be ready for tomorrow...whatever your dreams may hold.

Through discipline, education, and developing the best habits, you can take advantage of how the stock market can help your income grow. There are few things more rewarding than taking control of your finances so you can live out your dreams on your terms, free of fear, and ready to flourish. I know from my experiences, there hasn't been a day that's passed by that I haven't been grateful for this in my life and now I help others find their groove within the market. It is so rewarding.

About Krystle

Krystle Hall enjoys helping people solve problems by utilizing a variety of techniques and unique strategies to achieve the best results. She launched her own business, **Stock Market Investing for Beginners**, to educate people on how to grow their finances for retirement.

Krystle coaches individuals on the steps they need to take in order to build wealth and reach financial freedom. Knowing where to properly allocate your resources is an important step in order to achieve the best return on your investment. With so much information out there showing numerous ways to save money, she was able to bridge that gap by teaching others how to grow their savings by investing in the market wisely. Her simple guidelines have provided her clients with lasting success and fulfillment in their lives.

Krystle earned her Bachelor's Degree and Master's Degree at the New Jersey Institute of Technology. She is also a member of the Financial Planning Association and the American Society of Association Executives.

Growing up in a family of CEO's and Engineers, Krystle Hall always had a knack for numbers. She excelled in the math and science field and worked as a Chemical Engineer for Fortune 500 companies. Working in the corporate world made her aware of the countless people that fear the stock market along with the lack of guidance people receive when it comes to retirement planning.

You can connect with Krystle Hall at:
- krystle789@gmail.com
- www.stockmarketinvestingbeginner.com

CHAPTER 9

CONQUERING YOUR DEMONS TO ACHIEVE SUCCESS

BY PATRICK JINKS

Limits, like fears, are often just an illusion.
~ Michael Jordan

Some of our obstacles are real. Life throws real challenges at us. Not every obstacle can be defined as something merely "in our heads." We need skill, perseverance, help from others, or courage to step outside of our comfort zones in order to overcome some challenges.

Perhaps you have heard that courage is not the absence of fear. Rather, it inspires action DESPITE fear. On the other hand, it is not appropriate to push through everything we fear. Some fears are healthy. Fear is programmed into us to protect us from certain things. It represents our "sixth sense", which warns us to steer clear of trouble.

Many of our issues, however, are only there because we allow them to be. We BELIEVE them to be. One of the most restrictive feelings we can entertain is the fear that they MIGHT be real. From my simple perspective, fear of something is often related to a lack of knowledge. When I know something can harm me, I respect it more than I fear it. Some examples are: fire, the ocean, fast cars, and heights. I am not afraid of fire itself, but I respect its ability to harm me if mishandled. Living in angst with the unfounded fear that my home will catch on fire while I am on vacation would be a different thing.

In her book *Loving What Is*, Byron Katie shares four questions that can change your life. Asking ourselves these questions at the right moments can be transformative.[1]

1. Is it true?
2. Can you absolutely know that it's true?
3. How do you react when you think that thought?
4. Who would you be without the thought?

I have learned to ask these questions. In fact, I often ask the leaders I coach some version of them. Many of the assumptions leaders hold are founded in something other than truth. I hear things like:

- "I don't think my peers like me."
- "My boss doesn't care about the people in this organization."
- "I am terrible at social interaction."

Applying Katie's four questions opens windows of possibility. One of the best times to use questions like these is when we are experiencing fear of something. This is especially true when we fear the unknown, and our imaginations are getting the best of us. I learned this at a young age, in traumatic fashion.

> *The enemy is fear. We think it is hate; but it is really fear.*
> ~ Mahatma Gandhi

I am the baby of six children born to Clayton and Sandra Jinks. Dad was an officer in the U.S. Army. When I was seven, we lived in a pretty sweet, four-story officer's quarters at Fort Benjamin Harrison in Indianapolis.

I remember two things about the Fort Harrison house that were most impressive to me at the time. One was a bathtub so deep, you could practically dive in and not hit your head. The other was the basement. Mom and Dad decided the basement made a perfect play room for my youngest sister and me. It kept us out of everyone's hair, and we could be as loud and messy as our childish hearts desired.

I needed only a few things to build the greatest kid fort ever built. I

---

1. Katie, B., & Mitchell, S. (2002). Loving what is: Four questions that can change your life. New York: Harmony Books.

arranged some old wooden tables on their sides along with some unpacked moving boxes to frame the rooms. The finishing touch was my masterful spreading of our abundant supply of green and blue army blankets and furniture pads for the roof and additional room dividers.

My fortress filled the entire basement, giving my sister and me countless hours of adventures. It was a fort inside a fort — at least to a seven-year-old boy with a sizable imagination. It was also the talk of the family. Everyone knew how proud I was of the fort, and it was difficult to call me upstairs for dinner, a bath, or bedtime. Little did I know what pivotal adventure awaited me in that fort.

> *Fear is the darkroom where the Devil develops his negatives.*
> ~ Gary Busey

Another key tenet of our family was that we were devout Baptists. Attending church on Sundays was non-negotiable. Packing the entire family into Dad's blue Plymouth station wagon on Sunday mornings was a ritual. I remember wearing my Sunday best and making sure my hair was combed to mirror Dad's own hair.

But on one Sunday morning, the plans changed. I was unaware, but evidently, I was to ride to church that morning with my older brother and sister in a separate car. When I walked out of my bedroom, ready to climb into the makeshift rear seat that Dad had built into the station wagon, I found the house empty. *Could they have left me? Really?* The car was gone, and I searched the house for human life, but found none. Then, the phone rang.

In those days, you could dial your own number from your own phone, hang up, and your phone would ring. I never understood the purpose, but playing around with it was fun. My older brother and sister did just that. They were in the house, hiding behind a sofa, making the phone ring. After many rings, I realized I should answer, since I believed no one else was home. When I picked up, so did they, from the phone behind the sofa. The conversation went like this:

"Hello?"

"Patrick, I am glad you answered! Are you okay?" my brother asked.

"Yes. Where is everybody?"

"We are at church. Somehow, we were all in such a hurry, we didn't notice you weren't in the car."

"Well, what do I do?"

"It's okay. We are coming back for you. Hang tight."

"Okay."

"But there is something you need to do before we get there, and it's very, very important."

"What?"

"Well, we were just talking to Pastor Eveland. He said the Lord told him that there were evil spirits in your fort, and you must go downstairs and destroy it immediately! He said you couldn't wait for us to get back, or the spirits would find you!"

"WHAT?!?!?!"

"It's okay. He told us exactly what you need to do, but you must do it exactly like he said. Are you ready?"

"WHAT?!?!?!"

"You can do this, I promise. First, go downstairs and stand in front of the fort. Next, do you remember the song, *Rock of Ages*?"

"I think so," I replied, as my knees grew extremely weak.

"Okay. Good. Start singing *Rock of Ages* while you clap your hands. Then, turn around three times while you are still singing and clapping. Are you getting this?"

"I think so. When are you guys coming? Why don't you just come do it?" I was absolutely terrified.

"Because Pastor Eveland said only the person who built the fort can drive out the evil spirits. Plus, he said if you don't hurry, the spirits will make their way upstairs and get you!"

"What if I don't remember all the words?"

"That's okay. Sing the ones you know over and over."

I trembled. "Then what?"

"After you have turned around three times, you have to completely wreck your fort. Leave nothing standing. When you finish, come back upstairs and let us know. We'll hold on the phone while you do it."

"Are you guys sure? I am scared!"

"We are sure! You have to! Pastor Eveland promised the Lord would be with you."

> *We must travel in the direction of our fear.*
> ~ John Berryman

I worshiped my brother, and I trusted Pastor Eveland. I made my way down the dark, squeaky stairway to Hell, and stood before the Devil's lair. The evil spirits — I could literally feel them — were real to me. My brother (and Pastor Eveland) had spoken them into existence. My young mind knew no better than to let them.

I actually knew very little of *Rock of Ages*, but I belted out the line, "Rock of Ages, cleft for me — let me hide myself in Thee!"

I sang it over and over, while obediently and cautiously turning and clapping, trying to keep my eyes on the fort at all times. Three turns felt like ten. But I counted carefully, and when the third turn was complete, I lost all control on the fort. Kicking and tearing, yelling and flailing, I laid waste the former Camelot. My adrenaline shot me upstairs before any of the spirits could realize what had hit them. The one-two punch that the Lord and I had delivered was swift and accurate. As instructed, nothing was left standing.

When I reached the top of the stairs to the kitchen, I could hear voices laughing. My fear increased, as I was sure this was the mocking of the evil spirits that had somehow reached the top of the stairs before I had. But alas, it was my teen-aged siblings enjoying their mischievous handiwork.

> *Do the thing you fear most, and the death of fear is certain.*
> ~ Mark Twain

I beat the fear that day. My sacrifice of the fort was satisfying. At only age seven, I had stood and fought with courage to conquer my demons. Years later, as I shared this story with people, I realized that I had followed a formula of sorts to succeed at the fort.

First, I had to *__face my fear__*. I had to have the courage to acknowledge and face my enemy. Walking down the steps to the basement was the investigative action I had to take before anything else could happen.

Next, I had to *__mentally prepare__*. Standing before the fort, I went through the lyrics in my head. I pictured myself turning and clapping, and then destroying. I had to psych myself up.

The third step was to *__establish my competitive advantage__*. I had to apply the ingredients. I couldn't just start destroying the fort. I needed the tools that would leverage my action. The ritual of singing, turning, and clapping represented the difficult preliminary work of making sure I had the power on my side.

Finally, I had to act with commitment and conviction. There was no going back. "Leave nothing standing."

> *You always have two choices: your commitment versus your fear.*
> ~ Sammy Davis, Jr.

Fast-forward about 40 years. I was 21+ years into a career of nonprofit and community leadership. I loved my work, but longed for a coaching business of my own. Coaching was what I was best at. Like so many struggling to find the path to purpose, I wanted to take the leap, but I couldn't let go of the rope. The rope provided a steady salary with benefits, an established network, and a role that fit me comfortably.

What exactly was I afraid of? I will openly tell you! I was afraid I would fail. I was afraid I wouldn't make enough money to support my family. I was afraid I didn't have the tools and tricks that others had. I was afraid it would take too long. I was afraid I didn't know enough about marketing. I was afraid people would not want what I offered. I was afraid of embarrassment. I was afraid of falling short of the other side if I took the leap. And, I was afraid that if I did fall short, there would be no recovering.

Then it hit me. The evil spirits from Fort Benjamin Harrison had returned, with a vengeance.

> *How very little can be done under the spirit of fear.*
> ~ Florence Nightingale

Once I realized what was happening, I walked myself back through the four steps that had allowed me to vanquish my childhood nemesis.

Step 1). I decided to stand face-to-face with my fear, and acknowledged it. I applied the right questions, and identified the fear (a major turning point of any such battle).

Step 2). Next, I prepared myself mentally. I developed a mission and strategy, gathered a network of supporters, and prepared for business. This step included vision. I visualized my success. I envisioned my future business and the work I wanted to do.

Step 3). Then, I laid the ground work. I wrote content, developed facilitation processes, designed product, and studied marketing. I communicated with my potential clients, and put my business infrastructure in place. Then I made sure that what I was offering was unique, and that my pricing structure gave me a competitive advantage in my field.

Step 4). Finally, I acted. I put myself out there – imperfectly, but confidently. I decided that I would not treat this as a dabbling experiment, but rather as a life change. *This is what I do now*, I told myself.

Today is still an adventure. I remain guarded against realities, but I refuse to fear what isn't there. I talk to people on a regular basis who are still afraid to take the leap toward their purpose, and I share my secret 4-step warrior strategy with them:

1. Face the fear.
2. Mentally (and spiritually) prepare.
3. Establish your competitive advantage.
4. Act with commitment and conviction.

The only thing we have to fear is fear itself.
~ President Franklin D. Roosevelt

FIGHT THE GOOD FIGHT, AND KEEP THE FAITH!

About Patrick

Patrick Jinks is an inspirational speaker, trainer, facilitator, author, and most of all, coach. Patrick's company, The Jinks Perspective (www.jinksperspective.com) helps leaders and their organizations achieve clarity, simplicity, and alignment in their work.

As an award-winning professional photographer, Patrick learned the value of viewing challenges through the right lenses to achieve success. His unique, fresh approach to strategic planning and leadership coaching takes organizations beyond the tired, conventional planning processes that produce little value.

After a successful 21-year career in nonprofit executive leadership, Patrick "changed lenses" to serve the sector from another perspective. Today, he coaches leaders in both the social and corporate sectors, from local to international organizations. He serves his clients through the lens of a coach rather than a consultant, drawing out and elevating the best thinking of his coachees, instead of prescribing one-size-fits-all solutions.

Based in Columbia, SC, Patrick is a member of The Forbes Coaches Council, and he is a regular contributor to Forbes.com and TrainingIndustry.com. He is a certified adjunct executive coach and trainer with Leadership Systems, Inc., and a certified *Influencer* trainer with VitalSmarts® (the group that brought us *Crucial Conversations*). He is a two-time training award recipient from the Association of Talent Development (formerly known as the American Society for Training and Development).

Patrick has served as adjunct faculty at Millersville University's Nonprofit Resource Center in Lancaster, PA, and United Way Worldwide's Center for Community Leadership in Alexandria, VA. He is a past president of the Blue Ridge Institute, a national consortium of social sector executives, and has keynoted at regional and national conferences, including the Global LEAP Coaching Summit.

Success Starts Today is Patrick's second collaborative project with Jack Canfield. He co-authored *Taking the Leap: How to Build a World-Class Coaching Business* with Canfield, and other world-renown coaches, such as Marshall Goldsmith, Cherie Carter-Scott, and Mark Thompson. Patrick is also the author of *Strategic Fail: Why Nonprofit Strategic Planning Fails, and How to Fix it.*

CHAPTER 10

ACHIEVE

BY DR. KATHLEEN ALLARD-WASAJJA

*We have two lives, and the second begins when
we realize we only have one.*
~ Confucius

With time, experience and dedication, the quality of your life should be going up, not down.

If you could create a second life, what would it look like? What are you craving? If you're thinking: "Well Kathleen, there are so many things that I can think of," that's great because you're the person I had in mind when I wrote this chapter.

Whether you want more time for yourself, or more time with your family, to start a new career or business, to improve your health or to try new things, you have a desire that's been building and building to change your life.

When you realize that you have only one life to live, your second life can be much more fulfilling, because it's now focused on being yourself, cherishing the time that you still have with your loved ones and finally enjoying life like you never have before.

I want to encourage you to develop and monetize your talents and gifts. In today's uncertain economy, the more income possibilities that you have, the more freedom and ease that you have to adapt and move from where you are to where you want to be.

My goal is to provide you with actionable strategies, the ones everyone should know, to help you achieve your goals, overcome the obstacles that leave people feeling stuck, and learn how to use your fears to help you improve. If this sounds good, then:

Here you go. . . enjoy!

Open your mind and let the success strategies walk in

To begin with, invest time into doing new things and activities that you enjoy to gain more clarity on who you are, what you really want (it's not what other people think you should be doing), what you need and what you can give back to help other people achieve their goals, using your unique gifts and talents.

Remember that all of the areas of your life are important and every area of your life influences another. Therefore, you need to give your attention progressively to all of these areas of your life:

- personal life
- professional life
- family
- relationships
- health
- finances

Having only one or two successful areas in your life can create issues in the other areas, such as dissatisfaction, unhappiness, and stress.

Even though we can't control all of the stressful situations that develop in our lives, or their outcomes, investing time to figure out solutions to improve our circumstances is important.

Getting started today...the ultimate goal: Achieving Results

Did you know that recent advances in neuroscience have shown us that the brain has an extraordinary ability to continue learning and modifying our behaviour through a concept known as "brain plasticity"? For anything you think that you can't do, keep in mind that by learning and practicing, you can get better by adding success strategies to your schedule every day.

Your brain is closely connected to your body, which is why taking care of your health through exercise and eating nutritious foods can give you more energy to achieve your goals.

Setting yourself up for success: Working on a new and improved you

Just like other body parts, your brain can also be trained to perform better.

Let's look at four of the most common limiting factors to success, and learn how to overcome them:

1. Lack of energy
2. What other people think
3. No roadmap: No clear vision of what you really want and why you want it
4. Goal-related fears

Let's start with:

1. Lack of energy

Problem: Many people feel tired and stressed, so they don't invest time into changing their life. Keep in mind that doing what you are passionate about is actually a great energizer.

Checklist: Strategies to overcome a lack of energy

(i). Invest in your health by starting to juice fruits and vegetables once or twice a week, and build your way up. Juicing can boost energy levels, help you feel younger and maintain better health and weight. Search online for easy, delicious juice recipes. Buy them if you can't make them.

(ii). To quickly repower your energy, take short naps.

(iii). Your to-do list shouldn't look like you're running the country because it can lead to stress and procrastination! Decrease your list, delegate what you can, and slow down to gain more ideas, time, and focus.

2. What other people think

Problem: What other people think has a huge impact on our capacity to make changes. Many people, even high achievers, avoid doing something that they know would benefit them because they are concerned about the reaction of the people surrounding them.

The desire to want to "fit in" is normal; it gives us a sense of security. This need lies deep in our subconscious mind, the part that controls our beliefs, habits, actions, memories, personalities, and behaviors.

Obviously, other people's opinions can be insightful, but it's important to follow what feels best for you and take control of the direction of your life.

What appears to be consistent in the human experience is the need to live a life that has more to do with who we really are and what we truly want to experience.

Here is one insight from a select group of terminal adults, addressing what they would do differently if they had more time to live: (from *The Top Five Regrets of the Dying: A Life Transformed by the Dearly Departing*, by Bronnie Ware).

- "I wish I'd had the courage to live a life true to myself, not the life others expected of me."

With this in mind, listen to your "inner voice" and make sure that you are living a life that is all about what you really want.

Checklist: Strategies how to overcome what other people think

(a). Connect with people who have achieved what you want to achieve.

Connect with trustworthy, high achievers right now who have reached the goals that you want to achieve. They can make a huge difference by giving you more ideas, helping you overcome obstacles, and referring you to other people who can help you. Find these people through associations, masterminds/mentors, retreats, group coaching, referrals, entrepreneurial organizations, and, of course, everyday life.

Think of offering them value by letting them know your areas of expertise; they might appreciate your help in the future.

(b). Be selective as to what you say and to whom you say it.

If you are making significant changes in your life, expect that some of your family, friends, or colleagues won't understand and support what you're trying to do. It's not even a question of if it happens because it will, and some people will never "get you". Be selective as to what you share and with whom.

(c). Consider coaching.

Most successful people have coaches because coaching (private or group) and mastermind groups can significantly increase their chances of reaching their personal and professional goals – and doing so faster – by creating structure, generating ideas, and enforcing accountability for the work that they are already doing.

(d). Let go of your "secret hopes."

Let go of your "secret hopes" that everyone will like you

or what you do. Here's why: no matter how much good you bring, you will always have people who are negative and unable to bring constructive comments. Protect your energy with the support of positive high achievers.

(e) Invest time in your personal development.

Increase your personal development education time instead of your entertainment time; spend more time and money "in yourself," instead of "on yourself"(clothing, electronic items, etc). Read books or watch personal development videos, and if you do this during your trip to or from work, you won't need to set aside extra time for this task.

Put into action what you learn right away, and make a habit of evaluating the quality of your day, every day, and make the changes that you need as you go along.

Learn from people whom you admire and read the biographies of the challenges of successful people. I, myself, was greatly influenced by Jack Canfield, and I'm so grateful. As you read through this book, consider following the authors who inspired you the most.

In addition to coaching, masterminding, or mentoring, other methods that can help if you have limiting beliefs and fears are hypnosis and the Emotional Freedom Technique (EFT).

Note: If you have a history of psychological disorders, or have an unstable life or health condition, always refer to your health care provider.

3. No roadmap, no clear vision of where you want to go

Problem: Not knowing what you really want to do, or not having a specific plan to get there.

Many people don't have a clear vision or roadmap of what they want in their lives because they are busy and don't think about what else they could be doing to monetize their gifts and talents, other than what they are doing in their current careers. Being in control of the direction of your life is the result of thinking and creating possibilities.

One of the most common situations I encounter with my coaching clients is a misalignment between what is really important to them(values) and their current life choices. For instance, people who value family life as a top priority may stay in careers that no longer allow them to have quality time with their families. Chronic misalignment can lead to unhappiness, frustration, health issues, and of course, missing out on your own life.

Your values are those things that you believe are important to live by; they can help you make better decisions. When your life choices align with your values, you feel more confident, fulfilled, and happy.

Checklist: Strategies to gain a clear vision of your life

(a). Take the time to get clear on your values.

Becoming crystal clear on your personal values is a critical step because you'll easily notice how choices in different areas of your life either align or misalign. Being clear on your top values can help you make daily decisions and say "no" to those things that don't align with your values and life goals.

(b). Exercise 1: Value exercises by Kathleen Allard-Wasajja.

Go online and search for a list of at least 30-50 values, and print it out. Some examples of values are: creativity, freedom, achievement, adventure, challenge, and security.

Circle the ten values that most resonate with you. Now, bring your list down to your top five values, and then down again to the three most important values. If you hesitate, listen to your "inner voice." Next, look at all the areas of your life and determine: (i) which current life choices align with your values, and (ii) which current life choices don't align with your values and will need to be changed.

For example, one of my most important values is freedom. If you're like me, ask yourself:

- What does being free mean in each area of my life: personal, professional, family, relationships, health, and finances?
- What current choices allow me to feel free?
- What choices don't allow me to feel free and need to be changed?

Some of your values may change with life experiences. Repeat this exercise whenever you're not experiencing what you want in your life, or when you are going through transitions.

4. Goal-related fears

Problem: You have goal-related fears that may be preventing you from taking action: fear of success, fear of inadequacy (not being good enough), fear of vulnerability (exposing your true self), and fear of failure.

Goal-related fears can be a natural performance enhancer. Use your fears as a way to learn to improve yourself by programming your mind to find manageable solutions and get support from experienced people. The more you work on overcoming your fears, the easier it gets to find solutions to overcome them.

Checklist: Strategies to overcome goal-related fears

(i). Start by thinking about what you will gain by overcoming your goal-related fears.

(ii). Ask yourself:
- "What am I afraid of?"
- "Why am I fearful of this?" Ask yourself again: "Why?" and then another: "Why?" You can gain more clarity on the nature of your fear.
- "What can I do to overcome this fear?" Do you need more time to think about it, more practice, more help, more information to make a decision, to decrease the

size of the goal? To find all of the possible solutions, brainstorm alone and ask helpful people for their ideas. Get more information, help, or support. This process can help put your mind at ease, "knowing" that your fears have solutions.

Connect with high achievers, establish small goals to start off with, and always remember that other people's talents can help you reach your new goals, just as your talents can help other people reach theirs!

About Dr. Kathleen

Dr. Kathleen Allard-Wasajja is a medical doctor, a personal and professional coach, a hypnotherapist and a speaker.

If there's a life that you crave.... Dr. Kathleen Allard's passion is to help midlife, Generation X (born in the 1960's, 1970's and beginning of the 1980's) women and men, create their ideal life, with actionable strategies to: transform their personal life, create a new career or business, and improve their health.

She believes that there's no better time, with the experience that you've gained up until now, to learn how to move away from stress and fear. At midlife, the quality of your life should be going up, not down.

Founder of a personal and professional wellness development and training company, Vitality Leadership Group, Dr. Allard helps midlife Generation X (born in the 1960's, 1970's and beginning of the 1980's) women and men overcome goal-related fears and obstacles to achieve important life goals.

Dr. Allard's focus is on giving value to her clients by training them to achieve high-level mindsets, as well as thinking and problem-solving skills. She believes that in today's economy, investing more "in yourself" to create a stronger personal foundation, can bring more opportunities and freedom to move from where you are to where you want to be.

Dr. Allard brings a unique approach to personal development through her signature programs, *Achieve Method and Successful Life Strategies*. She offers live transformational retreats, coaching, and online courses to design and support a customized plan for each of her clients.

Dr. Allard specializes in clients seeking change, both internally and externally – the "mind, body, spirit" triad – to facilitate their transition from yesterday's reality to tomorrow's fulfilling possibilities. As a member of the Generation X demographic, she is passionate about reconnecting women and men with their core values – the ones that should always be guiding our choices to create the life that we crave.

In addition to her medical training, Dr. Allard is a professionally trained personal and professional coach, US-certified hypnotherapist (National Guild of Hypnotists), and speaker member of the National Association of Experts, Writers and Speakers in the US. She is certified in radio and television broadcasting and is fluent in both French and English.

Dr. Allard is also a John Maxwell Team Member, providing transformational training to organizations with her program, *Successful Leadership Strategies.*

Dr. Allard has over 15 years of experience as a physician (MD), practicing family medicine in Canada, has a background in emergency medicine, is a US board certified Integrative Medicine Specialist (conventional and natural medicine), and holds a Bachelor's degree in nursing. Dr. Allard's studies in medical school earned her the Rhône-Poulenc Award of Excellence in neurology.

With the experience from thousands of pediatric and adult medical consultations, caring about the life stories and supporting the success of people from all walks of life, she believes in the power of thinking from multiple angles to find solutions that improve our circumstances.

Dr. Allard also supports several charitable organizations. A dedicated athlete, she creates exercise plans for those whose injuries require adaptations. She enjoys reading, swimming, and sailing.

For more information on how to bring your life to a higher quality level, contact Dr. Allard at:
- www.vitalityleadershipgroup.com.

CHAPTER 11

A DOLLAR AND A DREAM

BY PRESTON PICKETT

You are not here merely to make a living. You are here in order to enable the world to live more amply, with greater vision, with a finer spirit of hope and achievement. You are here to enrich the world, and you impoverish yourself if you forget the errand.
~ Woodrow Wilson

The real journey began in March of 1973 when my parents Sandra Lynn Pickett and Preston Garnell Ayres conceived me. I am the second child of three. . . the middle kid. . . the one who had to fight for attention my whole life from my parents. The oldest seems to always get the guidance and the youngest is the baby, so we all know babies need extra attention, care and guidance. So, let's begin and take the journey with me up to this point in my life and why I feel I was sent here to accomplish God's will. (FAVOR). I truly believe we were all sent here on a mission to use our special gifts and talents to make the world a better place after we're gone. It's not about how many possessions or toys, cars, houses, money, etc., that we have, but what you did with the gifts God blessed you with. And I don't want to discriminate against any religions here – whether Christian, Jewish, Chinese religions, Muslim, Buddhist, Catholic, etc. I feel we all serve the same God and higher power, and practice the same principles to bring us guidance and wisdom.

I was born March 26, 1973 in North Philadelphia at Abbots Ford Projects. My father is Preston the 2nd, I'm Preston the 3rd. He lived in Norristown. My mother, Sandra L. Pickett, was raised in Philadelphia but born in

Memphis, TN. During the war, my Grandfather on my mother's side and my great uncles traveled to Philadelphia and brought all the ladies with them, and that's how we began to call Philadelphia home. So, somewhere deep down in my genes, I'm really a southern boy – like my hero, Ray Charles.

Once everyone got to Philadelphia, the ladies began having babies and the family tree up north had begun to grow. I had aunts and uncles from all over the City. During the 70's, it was hard, we moved around a lot. My father met my mother in Norristown and my older sister, Candice Pickett, was born. My father was a little bit older than my Mom by 5 to 6 years. My mom lied to my father and told him she was a little bit older than she actually was and they started dating. Once my grandmother found out, she confronted my father. What happens next was very sad and might have been the beginning of the end of having a two-parent household. My grandmother called my father over to the projects where my mom stayed and where my dad frequented a lot, partying and hanging out with friends. The word got around that a 21-year-old man got her 15-year-old daughter pregnant.

My grandmother Christine Smith was furious. My grandmother had lost my oldest uncle, who was murdered, at a young age. She drank a lot and was never well after that. Getting back to my father. He came over to the one-bedroom apartment. My grandmother politely asked him to sit down on the couch in the living room. She put a pot of grits on and spoke to him very nicely; she asked my father why did he get her 15-year-old child pregnant. He had no answers. As my mother sat there in shock, off the stove comes a pot of hot grits on my dad's lap. I can't even imagine the pain. My dad screamed as the skin from his stomach melted away. I guess a lesson was learned, but I don't wish that on my worst enemy. After two years, my mother and the family made up and then I was born. I was born at Women's Medical Hospital right across from the projects where we lived in North Philadelphia.

We jumped around from house to house. My grandmother and mom did not get along after a while. They could no longer see eye to eye. The drinking was out of control and it was time to move on. By then, my Grandfather Eddie Pickett had re-married. His wife was a strong Christian woman from down south who had migrated up north to New York during the Sugar Ray Robinson days when the City was vibrant and booming, and people were coming home from the war. She eventually moved to Philadelphia and met my grandfather.

They were a match made in heaven. She became the strong matriarch of the family and was very stern. She is currently around 94-years-old and still living. I credit her for a lot of my strength, success, Faith and upbringing. She taught me so much. She has great values, for one she was a Christian woman; secondly, she could cook her behind off; third, she kept the house immaculate, and lastly, she was great with money and kids. My mom became very rebellious during those years. My mother would go to her for loans and help from time to time. But she hated that my mom was in the streets drinking and smoking and eventually doing drugs. So, she came down on her pretty hard and my mom shut down.

The drug problem increased and our world was turned upside down. Fast forward to The Angora Terrace days of the early 80's. We finally got a home to live in, 5538 Angora Terrace, in southwest Philadelphia. Finally, I would make friends and be a normal kid. We had a great upbringing. We had all the best things life could offer, at least we thought so. My mother was eventually murdered in May of 1985. Still to this day, it was the worst day of my life. I cry every time I think about it. I thought the pain would go away but it hasn't. There is not a day that goes by that I don't think about my mom, but I'll keep the story brief.

I was attending Bartram High School Freshman Center. We got out of school that day and I went over a friend's house to chill like we always did. A friend of mine named Micah Solomon ran around and got me. He said the cops are at your house. I never could have thought in a thousand years that my Mom would be murdered. We ran through the south west near Whitby Ave, up through Frazier St, over the train tracks through the mud on a rainy day, then through the alley way on Angora Terr. And cops were everywhere. My heart dropped. People ran up to me and took me to the porch.

That's when the officer started to tell me, but before he could get it out, I saw my sister running up the street screaming. I went deaf. The words now came out really slowly, "Sorry son, your mom has been murdered." I never forget sitting on the steps when my father came down from Norristown. Everyone was crying. We sat on the stoop. Candy and I were going with my dad and my younger brother Gerald "Raheem" Pickett was going with his father to NJ. I was heartbroken.

But I still remember to this day a voice spoke to me. 'You have two options. You can be a Success or you can put your tail between your legs and be a failure.' I sat there while my dad was trying his best to take all three of us with him. A spirit came over me and a little voice said, 'It's time to grow up and be a man—at 15.' I promised myself and my Mom that I would make something of myself and be a SUCCESS.

REAL ESTATE — THE NEXT CHAPTER

The do's and don'ts to becoming a Success.

As I attended Penn State University, I did what every college kid does. I partied like a rock star, dated, had fun and then had more fun. I met a lot of great people, but couldn't get into my Major of Marketing at the Smeal College of Business due to not taking calculus in High School. I was up late one night studying Economics and Statistics, drinking coffee. Carlton Sheets came on the television. Ah-ha? The light bulb clicked on. If Labor and Industrial Relations don't work out. This is it. That's my way out. If this school stuff doesn't work out and I have to go to those dreaded job conferences at the Bryce Jordan Center with all those people standing in line with resumes, I just couldn't bear the pain.

So, I thought, I would start going in the opposite direction from the crowd. "Real Estate" . . . it had a nice ring to it. Plus, I always wanted a great life style and a lot of kids one day. I knew this career would allow me to live the lifestyle I wanted. I went home that Thanksgiving to my girlfriend at the time who is now my wife, Christina Gresham. I told her father what I was planning to do but didn't have the money.

By the time school let out that summer semester, Mr. Gresham had ordered the kit and left it in the closet. I asked him if I could have it since he wasn't using it. Fresh in the box, I took it to my grandmother's house on Tulpehocken St. in West Oak Lane and dove in. My Aunt Sylvia would peek in my room from time to time to see what I was reading.

I then bought my second Ron Legrand book. By this time, it was not as easy as they say it is. It's a huge learning curve if you're not gifted with some of the talents you need to buy a property. Fear was a huge factor.

What if I lose it all, go bankrupt, get laughed at. A lot goes through your mind of why you should quit early, but for some reason, I have a high tolerance for pain. I dove in, I couldn't resist that itch. Fast forward to 2002. My wife and I were living with her parents and this Real-Estate thing just was not working yet. I didn't have any entrepreneurs in the family; no one knew a lot about business, let alone investing in Real Estate.

Then my first child was born, Olivia Symone. My beautiful little Princess, and my wife and I just got married. We had to do something. My stepmother at the time, Ms. Lisa Franklin, gave me about $500 spending money and gas. I owe her my life. And I had enough money to go to my first conference on how to make $3,000 to $5,000 flipping properties in 30 days. What did I have to lose? I drove all the way to Cleveland, Ohio in our black Honda Accord. Up the Philadelphia Turnpike to the Ohio Turnpike, then on to Cleveland. I left Poplar St. in Norristown around 6 pm. I had about $300 in my pocket and there I went. I got there the next day around 7 am, driving all night. I didn't have money for a hotel, so I slept in my car.

The information from the speaker, Cam Dunlop, was incredible. The next day, a gentleman asked where I was staying at? I was embarrassed at first, then I told him. He offered me to stay in his room for free, and had an extra bed. I got a good night's rest. And 'sure nuff' when I got home, I did my first deal for over $7,000. I was so happy. I moved my family out of my in-laws and we leased a home in the City.

Success! I owe a great deal to my first mentor, Kevin Scott. His words still ring in my ears today. "Only time something is hard Pickett, is when you make it hard." This meant 'keep it simple in the beginning'. When it comes to real estate, there is a right way to do things and there are wrong ways to do things. I was taught that real estate investing will always fall into four categories:

1. Wholesaling
2. Retailing
3. Lease-Options
4. Subject to/Owner Financing

My wife and I are currently the Founders of our second company we started after the first one collapsed after 'Great Depression - Part II' around 2008 to 2010. I've never experienced anything like it. We lost everything. Starting over again, PFR Investments LLC is a new company we formed. We are now a full-fledged company that has done hundreds of deals, including Wholesaling, Fixing and Flipping, Lease/Options, Mentoring and helping many people profit from Real Estate. We probably learned more from our failures than the 100+ deals we've done over the years. One thing about success is that you are going to fail in the beginning more than you succeed. Just as long as you don't give up.

> *Failure is success turned inside out.*
> ~ Anonymous

Where there is vision, there will be Provision. The journey is about Faith, following your heart and stepping out when you don't see the next step or the turn in the road. We are all constantly evolving and growing. With technology, the game of Real-Estate has changed since I started. If I can give any advice to the people reading this book/chapter who want to learn about Real-Estate Investing, it would be: Go get your licenses first, learn the basics. Even if you never become an Agent or Realtor at least you'll know the laws and what not to do, so you won't get in any trouble. Most agencies these days offer a Coach, Mentor and business plan, which is priceless. Mike Howell of Keller Williams is someone who has made it and took the route I am speaking about, we both have given advice to each other.

Secondly, with all the programs you see on TV, read the fine print. They make it look so easy. You really need guidance and someone who has been there before. It doesn't take $50-$100k mentoring programs or schools to learn how to flip properties. Go pick up a book, read on that certain topic you want to Master. I would recommend starting out Wholesaling, then work your way up to Rehabbing, working with a Hard Money lender first. You will learn a lot about Financing and how to buy right and what real rehab numbers are. They are there to guide you so you don't lose money.

Then you can try raising Private Capital to get money cheaper and move on to Commercial or whatever interests you. Still to this day, I have a Great Mentor (Mark), and a savvy coach (Ray) who is in five different markets. So, there it is. Without our Health and Family, we have nothing. Never, never, ever give up, no matter what anyone tells you, despite all the haters, fake friends, critics, people who try to compete with you and even people you help that turn their back on you. There's always another way around the wall, over the wall or through the wall.

It all comes down to: **HOW BAD DO YOU WANT IT?**

About Preston

Preston Pickett is currently the Founder of PFR Investments LLC, a Real-Estate firm in Pennsylvania, who specializes in helping Investors locate great deals, and also rehabbing dilapidated houses. He also volunteers his time in and around the community. Mr. Pickett has traveled all over the United States for intense training in: Raising Private Money, Foreclosures, Rehabbing, Retailing, Fundraising, Lease/Options, Coaching and attended Orleans Technical College for Construction (2014).

Mr. Pickett has a passion for working with Kids, Homeless Veterans and the Elderly, and has received letters from the Congress of the United States asking for assistance with the mission of our Veterans. He was the Director of Alliance of Empowerment in Housing and has also worked with non-profits in the area who caters to the homeless veterans in Philadelphia and around the United States. He also enjoys working with individuals and providing affordable housing.

The Mission at PFR Investments LLC is to Find, Fund, Develop and or Flip discounted and/or distressed properties to Real-Estate Investors, so they can choose from a wider selection for nice rehab investments or new construction.

Preston Pickett was born in Philadelphia March 26, 1973 and moved to Norristown with his father at the age of 15 when he lost his mother. He has two other siblings, an older sister and a younger brother. He attended Norristown Area High School from 1990-1992, where his father worked at Lukens Steel for over 20 years. Mr. Pickett married his high school sweetheart from Bishop Kenrick H.S and has three kids (Olivia, Preston IV and Myles).

Preston Pickett went on to attend Penn State University where he was on the Boxing Team and a member of Kappa Alpha Psi Fraternity. He was also President of M.E.C.C.A and Secretary of SGA. He majored in Labor & Industrial Relations and Minored in Business and African American Studies. After graduating from College, Mr. Pickett was the Vice President of Marketing at HomeVestor's and CEO of PGP Properties LLC, a newly-formed Corporation, where he was responsible for marketing, sales & acquisitions, and customer service. He also worked in the Mental Health Field as a Therapeutic Support Staff working with kids and adults who had Special Needs.

The Goal at PFR Investments is to give away 10% percent of all proceeds to their Church and to non-profits who invest in social causes around the region and world. They want to help: kids who lost a parent, Vets, the elderly, and cancer patients.

Preston Pickett's passion is to spread the knowledge of Real-Estate to all people who want to learn and benefit from the opportunities the Real-Estate industry has to offer.

CHAPTER 12

FOR GOOD HEALTH & SUCCESS, WE NEED NATURE IN OUR LIVES

BY DR. RITVA ELINA RUOTSALAINEN

At the youthful age of 19, I decided to study medicine, went to medical school and became a medical doctor. I have been a general practitioner for over twenty years, and I like my profession. I always get excited from advances and new discoveries in this area, and it is, of course, rewarding to help people with their health problems. For me, it has always been important to remember what my reasons for studying medicine were. I chose medicine because I was interested in human beings as a whole – both mentally and physically. It is a miracle how the human body and mind works – separately but together. I still get excited about the beauty of it. I learned many things in university, and after that, in my practice. I met so many people of different ages and in various situations. I learned also that there is still so much that we don`t know – yet.

My curiosity drove me to study hypnotherapy. When I learned hypnotherapy, I discovered exciting things how your mind and imagination can affect your body – they can affect your nervous system and, for example, decrease pain. This was something that I had not learned in school. For many reasons, medical education was, and still is, very much drug-orientated. Of course, drugs help to cure diseases and in many cases, makes lives better and last longer – but they cannot solve everything, and sometimes their side-effects are fierce – as we know from the problems with some painkillers. Drugs are good as one tool.

Why not use other tools more? Human health is affected by so many things: healthy food, exercise, adequate rest and sleep. We also need other people – their nearness, for safety, to dialogue with them, and for us to grow and develop.

I continued my studies for some years on mindfulness-based cognitive therapy (MBCT). Mindfulness practice is a technique where you practice how to slow down, and bring your attention into the present moment. It is being aware of the things that are happening at present – to feel the present through your senses. The human mind has a tendency to wander back and forth into the past and the future, and sometimes gets stuck in bad feelings or habits. It is a kind of "mind gym" to give you tools to be more present, aware, to concentrate, and be clear minded and able to choose how to react. Also, we can be guided to be aware of our behavior patterns and those unwanted things that we do on autopilot. It is based on old meditation techniques and used in different mental therapies, and coaching and research is being conducted in this area. I liked the practical approach of MBCT to mental problems, and the fact that mindfulness itself could be taught to larger groups, and would give quite a simple tool for people to reduce stress and prevent problems.

During my MBCT studies some years ago, I heard from a new area in psychology where patients were taken in to nature as therapy. I learned that in Japan, doctors prescribe "forest baths" for patients. For me it sounded lovely, but a little ridiculous. What is there to find? Everybody can go in to nature if they want to, of course it makes you feel good. I could not see any link between my profession and this method. For me it was too obvious, I was too close to see it. For me, nature has always been a source of joy, but also a source of some kind of self-healing. If I am stressed or feeling low, I go back in to nature to feel better and get energy. It can be a park, forest or place where I can see natural water. I have also noticed that if I want to dream or get ideas, the best place to do so is in nature.

Spending time in nature is natural for me. As a member of my family, I was born in a small town, but we spent most of our holidays in nature. We took small trips to the seaside or countryside, we went fishing or picking berries or mushrooms in the forest, and spent summers in simple summer-cottages where nature really came to our doorstep. Sometimes we had some activities, but sometimes we just walked around and looked at what was happening and how nature was affected by the seasons. It was lovely. Being near nature feels very natural for me also as a Finnish person. In Finland, many people spend their leisure time in nature. Many of them also have summer cottages outside their towns.

I knew that this was something that I had to explore.

I sought some information from this area, and saw that there was not much to find from a medical perspective at that time. I found that also, in Finland, they had just completed a small study about how nature experiences affect one's health. In fact, the Japanese researchers that I had heard about had been to Finland. They were invited to tell about their "forest baths" and their research. They also had a meeting in Finland with a large group of experts regarding the health effects of nature. The conclusion was that some studies showed improvement and progress, but required further studies to be recognized as medical fact.

I wanted to know more. During the next two years, I went to meetings where I met people who studied this subject or were interested about it. I was always the only doctor at these meetings! I also read studies and books on the subject. Because it is new field of study, it also lacks common international concepts that help compare the studies. But the more I learned about this field, the more convinced I got that this was really important. Most of our human population lives in towns, and many of them have lost their contact with nature. In the modern world, people spend their time inside, or connected to their electronic devices. In Finland, a large majority of people spend time outside many times a week in green areas, but the situation is changing. One large study shows that even if people felt much happier in totally green areas than in cities, they did not spend their time outside. This indicates that people do not realize the effects of nature experiences. The importance of a green environment has to be studied more before it is too late. It is important for the politicians to know how to plan cities, and for the people to know how to increase their well-being.

Large population studies have shown that people who live in greener areas are more satisfied and had less depressive symptoms than people who live in more urban areas. Another study showed that those who live near greener areas enjoyed improved health, both mentally and physically. This correlation was stronger amongst elderly people, housewives, and people with a lower socio-economic status. Studies showed that people became less stressed, more focused and more creative in green environments. Their blood pressure and heart rates go down, and the levels of the "stress hormone" – cortisol – went down, and this can happen within 15 minutes. The effects get stronger when you spend a longer time in greener areas. Nature affects our autonomic nervous system which controls our breathing, heart rate, and muscle relaxation, so that it gets balanced and our body and mind gets relaxed. This is important, especially when we remember that according to WHO (the World Health Organization), mental and physical stress – with too small a level of physical activity – are the two most important reasons for premature death in western countries. And furthermore, studies show that people tend to get more exercise when they move around in green areas than in more urban areas.

In a memory test, a group that took a 30-minute walk in an arboretum received better results than a group that did not. There is also some evidence that being in nature increases the amount of so called helper-cells in the human body. In nature, people have more positive thoughts and they are more social and feel more connectivity to other people and to the environment. They also have less anxiety and aggressive thoughts. Some studies suggest that even pictures from nature can be effective. Patients who look at these pictures recover faster from operations, need less pain medicine, and feel less anxiety.

This year also, leading Finnish professors in allergology recommended that people should expose themselves to nature to help their immune systems. Immune systems need a variety of certain bacteria to work in the best possible way. Studies show that children with more diversity in their environment had fewer allergic reactions and less asthma than children who lived in more urban areas. Maybe urban environments with no green areas do not have enough diversity to keep our immune systems working normally? These experts suggest that also, there are some other diseases that make parts in the body exhibit mild inflammation, and which are rapidly growing. These may also have something to do with the absence of exposure to nature.

I think that my visits to urban parks and nature has been a kind of mindfulness all my life. While I am fascinated with the details and beauty, I really am present in the moment and use my all senses instead of living only in my head. And after that, I feel relaxed and renewed. It has helped me to cope with stress and problems, and maybe helped me to think better and clearer and be more creative. I feel better when I have spent time in nature. Before, I just thought that it was because of the fresh air and the beauty of nature, and because I was used to doing so. But now, I know that there is much more to it than that.

As I told you before, stress causes deaths in western countries. Our nervous systems are bombarded by simultaneous and rapid information both at work and in our free time – information that causes stress – and there is not enough time and space to recover from it. It causes health problems, but also problems with free time and work. We can be irritated and have sleep problems because of it, and don't use our full capacity at work. It seems that being in nature is restorative and stress-releasing for us. And it is free! In Finland, studies show that if you spent time – over five hours in a month – in nearby green areas, you get restorative effects. The same applies when you visit even deeper nature outside towns from two to three times a month. They tell also that the more time you spend in nature in your free time, the more restorative feeling you get, and the better is your emotional wellbeing. Some studies show that by spending a few days in the wilderness, the effects are more profound. In some places, gardens and green areas are also used to help to cure people from severe stress-reactions and depression.

So what can you do to use nature as a stress-releasing, restorative and healing element? The first step is to be aware of this effect. This is simple, and yet – as the studies suggest – the effect on your work, life and health may be huge. And it usually feels good!

I give you some clues to increase your "green-dose" in your life:

1. Increase "green" in your daily life. Put nature elements in your house and office. These are pictures and parts of nature, for example, plants in your house. Look out at the green views from your windows.
2. When you go to work or lunch, go through a green area if it is possible. You can sometimes maybe also eat lunch or arrange meetings at parks, gardens or places where there is a beautiful green view, trees or where you can see water.
3. When you want to get exercise, go to green areas and parks. Don't speak on the phone or listen to your headphones. Look around and

pay attention to those details that attract you.

4. Spend more free time outside – in a garden, park or forest. Meet your friends there or take your children with you. There are plenty of activities you can do, or you can just walk or eat lunch together.

5. Go sometimes – at least once a month – outside of your town to spend time in nature. If you don't know how to do it, seek some group that has activities there.

6. If you are tired, or in stress, go outside to a green area, choose places that please you and take a walk there and just look around. Notice how you feel before and after. If you don't know what kind of environment you like, look at different places. Many people like environments with water or trees.

7. Take your children into nature. Wouldn't it be nice if they would get these health benefits too?

8. If it is possible, sometimes spend a few days in nature/wilderness. You may need a guide or some education to do this, but it's worth it!

At the time of writing this chapter, we are celebrating a day for "Finnish nature." Our country is the only country to have that kind of day, and I am proud of that. Our nature is so beautiful and it gives us so much pleasure and health – in fact, it is vital to us in many ways. As a doctor, I want to expand my holistic view of human health; it includes not only the body and mind working hand-in-hand, but also the relationships with other people and nature around us.

About Dr. Ritva

Ritva Elina Ruotsalainen is a physician who wants to teach people that being in nature can help them stay healthier and happier – and sometimes cure faster. She thinks holistically about human health, and has always been keen on finding new tools to prevent health problems as well as help her patients with their problems. She thinks that the mind-body and nature are connected, and both influence each other by creating wellbeing or illness. We know that too much stress causes disease and can lead us to an earlier death. Because life is getting more hectic, and our nervous system is bombarded more and more by simultaneous information, creating high stress levels, we urgently need ways to restore our body and mind. Mindfulness and nature experiences are simple and natural ways to do this.

Ritva has studied medicine at Oulu University, Finland and has specialized in general medicine. She has also studied hypnotherapy, mindfulness-based cognitive therapy and sleep medicine. Ritva loves that her profession enables her to put all this knowledge together for the benefit of her patients. She has also been tutoring younger doctors. Ritva has over twenty-years of experience in public health, and thirteen-years of experience in the private sector. She has had patients from every age group with a wide variety of health problems – both physical and mental. In addition to prescribing drugs, Ritva also advises people how they can help themselves with lifestyle changes. Ritva now works as an entrepreneur. She guides individuals as well as groups to a better way of life.

In recent years, Ritva has oriented herself around studies about how nature-experiences affect people's health. Nature has always been a source of restoration and self-healing for Ritva and many people around her. She is very familiar with how to use different "doses" of nature in her own life. Ritva loves Finland's beautiful nature with all it seasons, and she is proud that Finland is one of the countries where nature, air and water are the cleanest in the world. Because of all of this, Ritva is passionate about this subject. She feels that everybody should learn how nature can help us, and that everybody, in whatever condition they are in, should have the opportunity to enjoy different kinds of nature-experiences. This potential should also be used more for treating disorders and for rehabilitation. Ritva wants to combine all her expertise to offer people the best ways to do this in Finnish nature.

You can connect with Ritva at:
- www.weinnature.com
- ruotsalainen.ritva@gmail.com

CHAPTER 13

WHY DO I DO THAT?

BY JUDITH A. SWACK, Ph.D.

Jane is an entrepreneur and a divorced mother of two. She came for Healing from the Body Level Up™ (HBLU™) treatment to improve her parenting skills and treat her binge eating. On the subject of eating Jane said, "I don't overeat during the day, but after I put the kids to bed, I go to the kitchen and eat several bowls of cereal and milk. I'm not hungry, and I don't even like cereal and milk. Why do I do that?"

For many years, Mark was the head of marketing for a Fortune 500 company. Having built a reputation and network over the years, and having recently gotten married, he decided to start his own company as a marketing consultant. Through his contacts in the industry, he was invited to present his ideas for bringing state-of-the-art marketing technology to several large companies. Strangely, he was unable to close a single deal. "Why can't I get any business?" he wondered.

The answer for Jane, Mark and many others is *unconscious self-sabotage!* It is very common for people to set doable goals for themselves and then find, to their surprise and dismay, that their behavior is inconsistent with their goals. People on weight-loss diets often eat what they know is bad for them. People who want to create healthy relationships often ignore red flags and find themselves in painful and unsatisfying relationships. People who run small businesses often have trouble charging for their services and collecting payment. Nobody really does this intentionally. This peculiar phenomenon is caused by a misalignment between the conscious mind and the unconscious mind, resulting in unconscious self-sabotage.

HOW DO THE UNCONSCIOUS MIND AND BODY GENERATE SELF-SABOTAGING BEHAVIORS?

The conscious mind is your *rational logical mind.* It is very concrete, linear, literal, and objective. **The unconscious mind** is the land of *emotion* (which is not rational), *imagination, memory, creativity, poetry, and metaphor.* It thinks in images, sounds, feelings, tastes, smells, and sensations. It is not literal like the conscious mind. It makes associations and reads meaning into things to understand what you are experiencing (and it is often inaccurate). **The body** is concerned with *physical survival and reproduction.* It values safety, good health, comfort, strength, food, sleep, rest, cleanliness, a nurturing touch, sex, etc.

Growing up, people have negative, even traumatic experiences, the memories of which get stored in the unconscious mind and body. These experiences trigger negative emotions, causing people to imprint damage patterns in the form of negative beliefs about themselves, the world, and even life itself. Emotions are energetic sensations felt in the body. (That is why they are called *feelings.*) The more strongly a person feels something, the more he believes it, even if it is not true. Because emotions have more energy than thoughts do, they influence/run behavior. This explains why people do what they know isn't right for them even though they know better. At that time, their conscious mind is not in charge. Damage patterns adversely influence our perceptions, reactions, and behavior in such a way as to make it difficult to achieve our goals.

THE FOUR D'S: DELETE, DISTORT, DENY, DISMISS

How do people manage to hold on to beliefs that are not true? A belief forms a lens through which all external information is filtered. Information that agrees with the belief gets through the filter, and the person sees it as validation, proof, or support for that belief. In other words one sees what one believes. Information that disagrees with the belief gets deleted, distorted, denied, or dismissed.

Example: Sally believed that she was "unattractive." She went to a singles activity with a friend. Her friend observed that an attractive man was smiling at her. Sally responded by: (1) claiming that she didn't see anyone smiling at her (delete), (2) denying that the man was looking at her (deny), (3) stating that if the lights were any brighter or if he got any closer he'd run the other way (distort), and (4) imagining the man asking for her phone number and never calling, or, taking her out on one date and deciding he doesn't like her, so never mind (dismiss). In any case, Sally's behavior toward the man was lukewarm and uninviting. At the end of the evening, Sally met no one and concluded that her belief was right all along (a self-fulfilling prophecy).

HOW DOES ONE IDENTIFY AND CLEAR NON-USEFUL LENSES?

Sometimes a tremendous amount of evidence contradicting a limiting belief can break the lens and allow a new belief to form. This is called "live and learn." But live and learn can take a long time, and may never happen. So it is important for people to begin to align their conscious mind and intentions with their unconscious minds by noticing when something is not working properly. Then they can evaluate behaviors, beliefs, attitudes, emotional reactions and end results by focusing on whether something is *useful to them* or not, rather than whether or not something is true. It may also help to look at the results others are getting and wonder what others believe that *is* working. It may even help to get honest feedback from others.

One of the ways I teach people to communicate with the unconscious mind, body, and soul is to use the technique from Neuro-Linguistic Programming of going inside one's head, asking an open-ended question about what the part that is running the problem behavior believes, feels, or is trying to accomplish. Sending the question echoing throughout the whole body (I call this an emotional CAT scan) will bring a quick response as follows:

1. Visual: a picture, a memory, a dream that you can see,
2. Auditory: a thought in words, a piece of music, a tone of voice,
3. Kinesthetic: a physical or emotional sensation felt in the body. (Sometimes there is a taste or smell response.)

It's easy to interpret an auditory response in words. Pictures or feelings may require more questioning.

Once we find the emotion/belief/pattern in the unconscious mind and body, we use a technique that works at those levels (some of which can be self-applied) to rapidly and completely release these patterns. Healing from the Body Level Up™ methodology can recognize many different types of patterns, how they are structured, and where they come from, and then treat the problem by selecting from a wide menu of techniques. These are Energy Psychology methods like EFT and similar meridian tapping techniques, Neuro-Linguistic Programming, EMDR, Hypnotherapy, Applied Kinesiology, Body-Talk, Yuen Method, The Emotion Code and the Jaffe-Mellor Technique, to name a few. (Note: Talk therapy does not work because it only treats the conscious mind.)

RESULTS

With Jane, I asked her to go back to the kitchen scene and locate where in her body she felt the negative emotion that happened just before she ate the cereal and milk. She felt it in the heart and recognized it was fear. I encouraged her to go deep and determine what the fear was about. We found that just a year earlier, Jane's widowed mother had been diagnosed with Alzheimer's disease. In that moment of diagnosis shock, Jane concluded that now she would have to devote her life to taking care of her mother. This would require her to give up her business, neglect her children, give up her relationship with her boyfriend, give up the time she took to exercise, eat, and sleep well, and in short, give up everything that gave her joy in her life. To cope with the pain of all the (imagined) losses, her unconscious mind compelled her to eat comfort food in the form of cereal and milk.

We treated the fears with Natural Bio-Destressing (a meridian tapping technique similar to EFT), the craving disappeared, and the binge-eating stopped. Reviewing the situation with her mother, Jane now realized that there are many resources available to them. She felt confident that they would find creative solutions to caring for her mother while balancing the other parts of her life. "So," Jane asked, "if I find myself eating when I'm not hungry, I should just go inside, ask what the fear is about and tap?" "Good idea," I replied.

With Mark, I asked him to step back into the scene of a sales presentation and become aware of any negative emotion associated with the scene. He immediately recognized that he felt pressure in his head. Interviewing the pressure feeling revealed two issues: an attitude problem, and a cultural brainwashing pattern.

The attitude problem was the belief that it's a salesperson's job to sell himself and convince people to buy things in order to make money for himself and his company. In short, Mark thought that the customers' job was to take care of Mark.

Having coached many successful salespeople, I told him that the top performers think of themselves as **educators and service providers** whose job it is to help people get what they need and want. *The focus is on the customer.* When a good salesperson helps people get what they need and want, their customers are happy, the salesperson feels happy for having helped them, the salesperson gets paid, the company makes money, and everybody wins!

The cultural brainwashing pattern was the idea that it's the man's job to support his family. Even though his wife was a business executive whose salary was equal to his, he believed that now that he was married, he had to cover his salary and hers so she wouldn't have to work. He feared that if he failed to do this, she would reject him.

After we adjusted the attitude and cleared the cultural brainwashing pattern, he went home and discussed the financial situation with his wife. They agreed to have regular budget meetings based on market and sales reality. Mark closed most of the business he pitched that year.

Sally treated herself for the belief that she was unattractive during my community education flirting class. She used the WHEE (also known as TWR) technique. (To perform this simple technique, hug yourself with your hands resting on your biceps. Then tap alternating for three minutes until the negative emotion disappears.) She started dating right after the class. After further HBLU™ sessions, Sally is now happily married with two children, and her husband uses HBLU™ too.

GETTING STARTED: THE HBLU™ 4-STEP SELF-HELP PROCESS

Step 1: Notice that you are not getting the results you want in a certain situation.

Step 2: Locate where in your body is the negative feeling you experience in that situation. Name the emotion. Ask that part of you why it feels that way.

Step 3: To release the negative emotion, use the Unwinding/Frontal Occipital Holding Technique: place the palm of one hand on your forehead and the palm of the other hand on the back of your head where it bulges out. Your head will move however it wants to and stop automatically when the negative imprint is erased in about 2-3 minutes.

Step 4: Think about the scene again. Notice what is different, and write down what you learned from the healing process.

Step 5: (Optional) – Focus on what you would like to accomplish, intensify the scenario to make it even more attractive, and use the Unwinding/Frontal Occipital Holding Technique to install the positive scene in your unconscious mind and body.

SUCCESS STARTS TODAY

Although this protocol is not a substitute for professional help, you'll be surprised at how much you can do yourself. Alignment of the conscious mind with the unconscious mind and body results in greater levels of inner peace, self-acceptance, and positive results in all areas of life. And, when you clear unconscious self-sabotage you'll find that although achieving your goals will still take work, it will take a lot less effort.

Copyright 2017 Judith A. Swack, Ph.D.

About Judith

Judith A. Swack, Ph.D., originator of Healing from the Body Level Up™ methodology, is a Biochemist/Immunologist, Master NLP Practitioner, Certified Hypnotherapist, Mind/Body Healer, visionary and leader in the field of Energy Psychology.

Dr. Swack has presented her dramatic results live on national television and at international conferences. She has published numerous articles in scientific, professional, and popular journals and authored the chapter "Healing from the Body Level Up" in the industry-defining publication, *Energy Psychology in Psychotherapy: A Comprehensive Source Book.*

Dr. Swack is a recipient of the 2015 ACEP award for major contribution to the field of Energy Psychology. She offers trainings both nationally and abroad. Dr. Swack has a private practice in Needham, MA. She and her associates offer individual client sessions in person, by Skype or by telephone.

For more information please see her website:
- www.hblu.org

CHAPTER 14

TURBOCHARGE YOUR SALES TRAINING

BY DANIEL MENDEN

"Pour me a Captain and Coke and make it a tall one please," Jared said to the bartender as he sat down at the bar outside the convention center at the Annual Dealer Meeting.

"Rough day?" his friend Matt asked.

"Rough day, rough week and a rough last six months ever since I became general manager of the dealership," replied Jared. "I knew it would be a challenge jumping from motorcycle sales manager to the general manager of the dealership but I never imagined it would be so frustrating and so hard to hit the numbers. I convinced the owner that I could do it if he gave me a chance but we just can't hit the numbers on a regular basis and I'm starting to get pressure to deliver. After ten years, I'm starting to worry I won't be there much longer if I don't turn things around."

"What's happening?" inquired Matt as he was getting concerned about his friend's obvious despair. He couldn't recall seeing Jared so frustrated ever before and the Annual Dealer Meeting is usually a time for optimism and having fun as the company rolls out the new model year motorcycles.

"We can't seem to hit the numbers in any of the departments including motorcycles sales and it doesn't help that I've moved to the GM role and stopped selling bikes directly. You know Geno, our top sales guy, he's even struggling in the current environment," lamented Jared. "I'm not sure what to do next. How are you guys doing this year."

"Well, it's been a tough market for us too but we've had pretty consistent improvement in our numbers across all the departments over the last 15 months or so," replied Matt. "In fact, we're on pace to have one of our best years in the last five years if we keep things going."

"How the hell are you doing that?" retorted Jared as he slammed his nearly empty Captain and Coke on the bar.

"It's been a combination of a new approach to training, linking dealership and individual goals and leveraging leadership to support the application of the new skills learned in the training," stated Matt.

"Every department in our dealership has goals and we're doing training all the time but it's not making a difference for us!" Jared replied as he picked up his glass and finished his drink.

"Let me buy you another one as I fill you in on the details of how we're taking a different approach to reaching our goals and how training has helped turn things around," offered Matt.

"I'm all ears especially if you're buying," replied Jared.

"Well, the bad-news is there isn't a magic pill or secret potion you can take. It's hard-work and it requires staying at it. The good news is that it wasn't dumb luck either so it's something that is repeatable," said Matt.

"What do you mean that it's repeatable and how did you get started?" asked Jared.

"We implemented several changes over a 2-3-month period starting about a year and a half ago and that's when we started to hit the numbers on a consistent basis. The things we did are things that any dealership can do, but it takes hard-work and persistence. There were several steps we took and it all started with adding a new twist to our sales training plan," explained Matt.

"We do a ton of training for both selling skills and new products! So, what's different about your sales training?" inquired Jared.

"First, it's probably more accurate to call it success mindset training instead of sales training. You know Jack Canfield? He wrote a book called *The Success Principles*. The training focuses on something not covered by most sales training. It builds new habits or a mindset of success. Things like taking 100% responsibility for your results, learning how to set and achieve stretch goals by using techniques on a daily basis like visualization and affirmations," said Matt.

"Sounds a little hokey to me. Does that stuff really work?" asked Jared with a hint of the Captain and Cokes kicking in.

"Call it what you want but it really does work. Most top athletes use visualization and affirmations to improve their performance," Matt said in a convincing tone.

"Okay, so you did this 'success mindset' training but it can't be just that. You said you did several things. What else? I need something more than that!" countered Jared.

"Oh, there's more. The success mindset training had everyone develop individual goals that were directly linked to departmental and dealership goals. Before this we told everyone what the dealership goals were and expected the employees to deliver without ever committing to individual goals," explained Matt. "Now we have goals that cascade from the dealership level all the way down to the individual level. That means the success of the staff members is directly linked to the success of the dealership."

"That's all nice to link the goals but how do you know what the individual goals are and if they're doing what they said they would especially for stuff like using affirmations and visualizations?" Jared responded. "So, what else happened?"

"Well, there is one more thing we did that really helped. It wasn't that hard but we never really knew before that it was so important. We got the managers more directly involved through a process the trainer called 'Leverage Leadership'," explained Matt. "This helped hold people accountable for implementing the new skills and habits."

"That sounds pretty good. How does this 'Leverage Leadership' thing work? Is that something I have to do?" asked Jared.

"Well yeah, it's something you 'have to do' but more importantly it's something your managers need to support. Apparently, there's lots of data that shows managers are a critical leverage point for getting people to apply what they've learned in a training class. I guess it makes sense but we never really put much emphasis on it in the past," Matt stated.

"What do they have to do?" Jared asked.

"We had a 'Leverage Leadership' session before the first module started with just the managers, so they could develop their own game plan as to how they use the 3 R's to make sure the program works," Matt replied.

"The 3 R's? It's getting more confusing by the minute" Jared blurted out. "What does that have to do with anything?" he challenged.

"It's actually pretty simple! It's Role Model, Reinforce and Recognize. The managers came up with their own plan as to how they would hold people accountable for applying and reinforcing the use of the new skills and success habits," explained Matt. "They committed to doing certain things to follow up with the employees and we review the plan periodically as a leadership team. This helps make sure we're walking the talk and recognizing our folks when they achieve some success. It's pretty simple stuff, but we never consciously thought about doing this before. It's something we need to work at doing a better job of whenever anybody completes any kind of training," Matt continued.

"The trainer also sent out messages in between the training modules with information and links to other websites that had information that reinforced or reminded everyone of the topics covered in the program. It really helped keep things fresh in everyone's minds and helped keep them motivated."

"The Leverage Leadership effort includes regular reviews of both dealership and individual results. It wasn't always good news but we were open and candid without being threatening when people didn't hit their targets. There was also something cool that came out of this. It was that everyone kind of rallied around the folks that may have been struggling and offered to help or support them if they could." Matt said. "In some ways, the whole program brought us closer together as a staff, which is something I didn't expect," he continued.

"So, this all sounds well and good so what's the catch?" said Jared.

"The 'catch'?" Matt asked with a puzzled look on his face.

"Yeah, the 'catch'. What didn't work? What's the bad stuff you're not telling me about?" Jared asked as he was digging for something bad about the program.

"Oh, the 'catch'. Okay, I guess the 'catch' is that it is hard work and the trainer isn't free. I wish it was as easy as slamming a couple of Captain and Cokes but it's not. It's something you and the entire team need to stay on top of every day to realize the results and success that you want. One of the things the trainer said was a quote from Jim Rohn that went something like, 'you can't hire someone else to do your push-ups for you'," explained Matt. "You have to stick with it every day so it just becomes the way you work and get things done. It doesn't seem like work after you do it for several weeks, as it just comes naturally because they're new habits," continued Matt.

"So, would you do it again?" Jared asked to test how satisfied Matt was with the program.

"Oh yeah, it was well worth it. Do you want the contact info for the guy we worked with?" asked Matt.

"Sure, why not. What we're doing now isn't working and what you described sounds like a lot better way to hit the numbers" replied Jared with a hint of a little bit of optimism in his voice.

"I'll tell you what. If this works for us like it worked for you. I'll buy the first round at next year's dealer meeting," Jared promised.

"The first round! How about you buy all night if this works!" protested Matt as he chuckled.

"We'll see, always looking for a free ride aren't you!" Jared said trying to limit the potential damage to his wallet.

Jared left the discussion with Matt with more optimism and reached out to the trainer. They soon started implementing the approach he had learned about from Matt. He quickly realized Matt was right about it being hard work, but it was also worth it as it was an effective addition to the training plan the dealership already had in place, and it helped improve the numbers as expected. He was feeling a lot better about the future of the dealership and his role as the general manager. Jared was looking forward to seeing Matt at the next dealer show and making good on the Captain and Cokes he owed him.

The story of Jared and Matt is a fictional tale but the elements of the program that Matt described in the story are based on tangible results from applying Jack Canfield's *Success Principles* in a dealership setting and other proven methods of driving performance improvement. The three key elements depicted in this story are summarized below:

1. Success Mindset Training – inspirational, interactive training centered on building success habits based on Jack Canfield's New York Times bestselling book, The Success Principles. Most sales training focuses on 'product' training or 'skills' training and overlooks including success-based training. Success training teaches sales people to take 100% responsibility for their results, no more blaming and excuse making. It teaches them other powerful tools and skills such as using visualization and affirmations as well as how to 'reject rejection' to name a few. Combining success training with product and skills training is a more effective and more powerful combination.

2. Link Dealership and Individual Goals – purposeful linking of dealership and personal goals. This assures that the success of the staff members is directly linked to the success of the dealership. All successful dealerships have clear top-level dealership and department level goals, yet many don't cascade those goals into individual level goals. Developing and connecting individual goals to dealership/department goals will drive higher levels of success because the employee's success will drive higher levels of success for the dealership.

3. Leverage Leadership – the leadership team develops their own plan to Role Model, Reinforce and Recognize the implementation of the success habits and to monitor results. There have been many studies completed that highlight the key role that managers play in ensuring effective application of new skills and knowledge. Yet, most organizations do a very poor job of supporting their employees

in applying what they've learned, so very often the new skills and knowledge get lost in the shuffle when employees return from training. The result is no improvement in performance. There are simple, yet powerful tools and processes that managers can deploy to set the proper environment before and after the training occurs, to ensure employees apply what they've learned and drive better business results.

Implementing this type of program can be accomplished in any type of sales organization, not just an automotive, motorcycle or powersports dealership. There are many examples of how a commitment to living the Success Principles will result in higher levels of business and personal success as evidenced by the following quote.

"I cannot begin to describe how this training has changed my life. Once I decided to fully commit myself and my time to this program I noticed changes for the better in both my personal and work life almost immediately. I wake up in the morning happy and looking forward to the day ahead and have more energy for the things that I WANT to accomplish. Thank you for giving me the ingredients I needed for the recipe to success and happiness in life!"
~ Stacie - F&I Manager at a Harley-Davidson Dealership in Ohio

There is no 'magic pill or secret potion' you can take as Matt stated in the story above, but better results are possible through implementing the three steps in a thoughtful and disciplined manner. You and your organization can realize higher levels of success than ever before with a new more powerful approach.

Is it time to 'Turbocharge Your Sales Training'?

About Dan

Dan Menden is an international speaker, trainer and consultant with over 20 years of success in helping organizations improve their performance. Having started his professional career as a high school then university level teacher, Dan eventually found his way into employee training and development at the Harley-Davidson Motor Company. He started at Harley-Davidson as a shop floor supervisor and that shop floor experience has never been forgotten as Dan always seeks practical, effective solutions to organizational performance problems.

While at Harley-Davidson, Dan was responsible for transforming Harley-Davidson University (HDU) dealer training into a matrixed global training organization that developed and delivered training to the 1400+ Harley-Davidson dealerships around the world. While Director of Dealer training, HDU deployed the biggest training initiative in Motor Company history as it delivered Harley-Davidson Customer Experience (HDCX) training to over 98% of the worldwide dealership network. The HDCX training initiative spearheaded the company's efforts to deliver excellent customer experiences across its dealerships. Dan also spent time working as a Performance Consultant for the dealer network and directly supported the Performance Group process – which helped hone a deep knowledge of dealership operations and financials.

Having retired from Harley-Davidson after 26+ years, Dan is now the Managing Director of Mensch Learning Solutions which is focused on helping its clients improve their performance through learning. In addition to his real world global training experience, Dan is a certified Jack Canfield Success Principles Trainer and a Certified Professional in Training Management (CPTM). Because of his background and experience, Dan is also an instructor for the CPTM program where he helps grow and develop other training professionals from a wide variety of industries from around the world. Dan has a B.S. Technology Education degree and a M.S. Management Technology degree both from the University of Wisconsin–Stout where he also taught as an instructor.

Dan's knowledge, skills and experience allow him to be effective in many industries with a wide variety of client needs including content development, training delivery, speaking, leadership coaching and strategy consulting. Having spoken with and trained groups from two-dozen to two-thousand, Dan is comfortable in adapting to meet the needs of the client from shop floor employees to the C-suite.

Dan can be reached at:
- dan@menschlearningsolutions.com
- Twitter: @Mensch Learning
- LinkedIn: Daniel Menden, CPTM

CHAPTER 15

YOUR GPS FOR FINANCIAL SUCCESS

BY ALISHA THOMPSON ADAMS

I recently spoke at a conference on the topic of *Mastering Your Money*, with a focus on the future. And as I contemplated the content of my presentation, the overarching theme – *"Focus on the future, and the future starts today"* – kept resonating in my spirit. Little did I know that my preparation for that conference workshop would serve as the foundation for my contribution in a book I would co-author with the great Jack Canfield... the very book you're reading today! Talk about serendipity!

If the truth be told, a financial mindset focused on the belief that **success starts today** is all about understanding the fact that succeeding in the mastery of our finances begins in the here and now. In other words, it begins today! And guess what? ... it begins with you and me! This is undoubtedly reflected in the two *success* principles I hold to be true when it comes to the topic of money. The first one being... *if you don't sacrifice for what you want; then what you want becomes the sacrifice.* And my other money truth is... *our financial success depends on the second letter in the word success: "u".* Simply put, your success in the arena of your finances is ultimately dependent on you; and relies heavily on you taking the bull (the *financial* bull that is) by the horns, and riding it until you achieve what you know rightfully belongs to you!

So, with the concept of *"my success financially not only starts today, but is totally dependent on me"* as the backdrop, let's explore the things we

149

can do now to ensure our financial success and prosperity are not only imminent, but epic as well. Now, I don't know about you, but I believe it's *time out* for us trying to guess, or *take a stab at*, what will ultimately assure us a financially successful and prosperous life. Therefore, in these next few pages, my aim is to provide a roadmap that unequivocally guarantees that the achievement of our financial success and prosperity is as much of a reality as the book you're reading. And to confirm I'm addressing the right audience; I just have to ask ... **Are you interested in taking this financial journey with me?** If so, buckle up, pay close attention and implement the suggested strategies. Ready? ... Set? .... **Here we go!**

Using what I call my Guaranteed Prosperity Strategy (GPS), the first stop on this financial ride is the **setting of our financial goals**. And let me say, anyone who has ever heard me speak, or is a personal client of mine, knows firsthand the importance I attribute to having financial goals. For I once heard it said that, *"the tragedy of life doesn't lie in not reaching your goals; the tragedy lies in having no goals to reach!"* How sad would it be to have that as the lasting epitaph of one's life! Not only that, I recall listening to a recording from Earl Nightingale (a pioneer in the study of personal success) in which he said, *"People with goals succeed because they know where they are going."* So, as we can see, financial success and prosperity today begins with the establishment of clear goals. As such, there are three things I want us to internalize as we prepare these financial goals. First of all, our goals need to be realistic; if not, we're setting ourselves up for inevitable financial failure. Secondly, a deadline needs to be attached to each goal; this provides a sense of accountability, and serves as a guidepost along our financial expedition. And thirdly, we need a plan... a **written** plan, that is. Simply put, we need a concrete playbook that offers a step-by-step approach for the achievement of our financial goals, by our established deadlines — *for a goal without a plan is merely a dream!*

The next destination on our financial success and prosperity trek is the **understanding of the importance of a budget**... better known as a *spending plan*. Interestingly enough, our financial goals have a major impact on our monthly budgets. In which, those financial goals we've previously established make up a good part of our budget, as budgetary line items. So much so, that when someone looks at our budget, they should be able to determine our financial goals at first glance. For example, a goal of *"retiring at the age of 55, with an $8,000 monthly income,"* could be reflected in our budget as a line item labeled: *"retirement fund."* Quite simply, a budget is an *estimate* of our income and expenses over a set period of time; and serves as a pre-established plan for our monthly spending. Wherein, the key is to know what's *actually* coming in (i.e., income), versus what's *actually* going out (i.e., expenses), on a monthly basis. And what I've found for the vast majority of my clients (as well as myself, many years ago) is that the *real* challenge is in getting a *firm* grasp on those monthly expenses.

Hence, if this is also a concern for you, then let me suggest that you commit to taking the same *30-day challenge* I issue to my clients (and have personally completed myself). So, for the next 30 days, write down everything you spend money on, regardless of whether it was paid for by cash, check, debit or credit card. And although I am not a gambler, I would be willing to bet you will be surprised at how much you truly spend monthly on those "innocent" (i.e., *inexpensive*) purchases. On a personal note, when I implemented the 30-day challenge in my finances, I was totally surprised by how much I spent on take-out (Ugh)! But, like me, refuse to allow it to discourage you. Instead, divert some (if not all) of those funds towards your financial goals and watch those goals come to fruition with lightning speed!

Continuing on with the successful mastery of our money; the next site on this financial voyage is the **creation of the "infamous" emergency fund**. Yes, you've guessed it; we have to make sure we have **no less than** 3 months' worth of our living expense money in a *liquid* account. And in today's uncertain economy, it would be an even better idea to have between 9 and 12 months' worth instead. In other words, when life hits (e.g., a necessary car repair, medical emergency, job loss, etc.); we need to be able to quickly access some funds (without penalty) to cover that unexpected expense, without fear that it will take us under financially. As a result, a retirement account is **not** an emergency fund. Instead, our emergency fund should be housed in a high-interest bearing savings vehicle (e.g., money market account and/or money market fund). There's nothing more comforting in knowing that when good old *Murphy* (as in the case of Murphy's Law) rears its ugly head with a surprise expense, we essentially have the funds available to handle it... without *"robbing Peter to pay Paul!"*

Now along this financial excursion, we cannot forget to **consider our credit status**. We've all probably heard the statement *"money makes the world go round."* Well, let me go on record as saying, *"credit makes the world go round"* as well! Which is why having no credit is often as bad as having bad credit. Why, you may ask? Because in this day and age, so much depends on others being able to verify our financial *"character"* – which is often based on how we handle our credit. Right, wrong, or indifferent… the truth of the matter is that the lack of a credit history makes it difficult for that *verification* process to take place; thereby ultimately resulting in a rejection. And just in case you didn't know, our credit history is used in the following instances (among many others): the employment process, opening a bank account, auto/home/personal loan approval, turning on of utilities, auto/property insurance rates and the issuance of credit cards.

Since our credit history is so important, it's imperative that we monitor what's being reported. Therefore, we should periodically check our credit reports. And the great news is we can do it for **FREE** at: www.annualcreditreport.com. This website is provided by the Federal Government, and allows us to get a free credit report, once every 12 months, from the three major credit bureaus (Experian, Equifax and TransUnion). However, keep in mind it's not enough to just obtain a copy of our credit reports, but we must also review them, and immediately dispute any errors found. Vigilance is the key to correcting and maintaining good credit.

Considering the fact that the second largest factor in the determination of our credit score (*payment history being the largest factor*) is based on our credit utilization ratio (i.e., how much of our available credit we're actually using), it makes sense that a good part of *considering our credit status*, involves getting out of debt. As such, the next stop on this journey to financial mastery is the **elimination of our debt**. The first step to a debt-free future is the decision to be debt-free. Once we've resolved to dump the debt, we have to figure out how much we owe, and to whom we owe it. After which, we need to determine which debt we want to pay off first, second, third, and so on and so forth. We can typically base this decision on selecting the debt that's either charging us the highest interest rate, or the one that has the lowest balance… the key is to select the method that provides us with the greatest level of motivation. And from personal experience, I've found that focusing on eliminating the debt with the lowest balance first helps to keep us encouraged along the debt-freedom drive. The essential ingredient in making this process work is that, as a debt is paid off, we should take 20% of that money that is now available, and put it into a short-term savings vehicle; while the remaining 80% should be put towards the next debt on our debt elimination list. Not only will we get out of debt sooner and cheaper than what we were originally on track for, but we will also build up a liquid cash fund for use in an emergency, or to fund our financial goals. Bear in mind, *debt freedom is a prerequisite to financial independence!*

Continuing on this financial expedition, we cannot neglect to **secure our retirement**. In this instance, we have to determine when we want to retire (i.e., the age), and to what level of income (i.e., how much money we want coming in on a monthly basis). This will help us figure out how much money needs to be in our retirement account by the time we want to retire. Realizing the earlier we start the retirement preparation process, the less we have to invest on a monthly basis. The other piece of this is to make sure we're investing the necessary amount of money in products that have historically outpaced inflation (i.e., the rising cost of goods and services) – whether that be stocks, bonds, mutual funds, index funds, ETFs, real estate, and/or collectibles. Since time and space does not allow a full review on this topic, I would highly recommend soliciting the advice of a trusted financial professional to determine the best investment strategy for you.

So, as we wind up our financial journey; we end where we began this discussion... recognizing the fact that we **have** to **start today**! For in the absence of doing so, we're basically procrastinating. Interestingly enough, I recently heard that *"procrastination is like a credit card... it's a lot of fun, until you get the bill."* Remember, you can do it today or regret it tomorrow... but you can't do both! ***SUCCESS STARTS TODAY*** – with the implementation of your Guaranteed Prosperity Strategy (GPS).

Here's to your success!

About Alisha

Alisha Thompson Adams is a financial expert whose career has spanned nearly two decades. Prior to entering the world of personal finance, Alisha worked extensively in the chemical engineering field, during which time she was introduced to the financial services industry. Soon thereafter, she walked away from a promising engineering career to pursue her passion in the financial arena; and she is thankful every day for having made that decision.

Today, as a licensed financial professional and Certified Financial Coach, Alisha focuses her time and effort on increasing the financial awareness of the public at large. Whether assisting individuals one-on-one with their personal finances, speaking at conferences, conducting seminars at churches, organizations, and corporations or educating male and female offenders in the prison system, one thing is certain... financial hope will be restored to those who cross paths with her. For no matter the venue, Alisha's primary emphasis is to ensure each person she comes into contact with grows financially as a result of the interaction.

Along with her love of financial education, she is equally as passionate about positively shaping today's youth into tomorrow's leaders. As such, Alisha enjoys the opportunity she's afforded to impart leadership principles into the lives of students through national and local programs. Without a doubt, equipping children to successfully compete in an ever-changing society is of paramount importance to her.

Alisha is the co-author of *Wisdom on the Wall*. She is a graduate of the University of Pennsylvania – School of Engineering. She was born and raised in Philadelphia, Pennsylvania and loves to dance, read, travel, and attend personal development programs. Alisha currently resides in Delaware.

Alisha is available for keynote speaking, financial education workshops, personal financial advising, and youth empowerment workshops.

You can reach Alisha at:
- contactalisha926@gmail.com

CHAPTER 16

WHEN STILLNESS SPEAKS

BY CHERYL IVANISKI, D.Ac., C.H., RDH

• A World of Doing

As human beings, we are always doing. Why are we always doing?

We attach sticky notes to our computers and leave voicemails for family, friends and others. We write emails, text messages, and activate the alerts in our phones as reminders. Some of us use the timers on our stoves, appliances and electronics. We write ourselves paper notes and use phone applications as reminders so we do not forget to do important items. These are all 'to do' lists.

Today, our lives are so full of checklists of things to do, that it can become overwhelming.

A typical list may look like this:

1. Pick up grocery store items
2. Fill the vehicle with gas / buy transit passes
3. Do laundry
4. Schedule hair appointment
5. Pick up dry cleaning
6. Take the kids to their activities
7. Schedule the teacher-parent meeting
8. Have family for dinner
9. Order online items

10. Work out
11. Check emails
12. Walk dog
13. Make lunch for tomorrow
14. Make Dr. appointment
15. Catch up on calls from work
16. . . . you get the idea!

Other things on our minds taking up space include thoughts from moments ago or yesterday, last week, last month, last year, 10 years ago, and experiences in early childhood. Perhaps you are thinking of a conversation, or reminiscing of a pleasant experience. You could be thinking of what is coming up tomorrow or next week. Much of this self-talk can also have a negative effect in our lives.

Think of the areas in your life:
- health
- finances
- relationships with family, kids, spouse, parents and others
- career change/downsizing at the office – thus creating more demand on your work load
- that upcoming presentation/report
- the vacation you want to take
- the raise or promotion you want
- that second job you are considering
- the kids' activities
- your fitness membership
- home maintenance
- hobbies, interests, and self-improvement

There are just so many things we do all the time. Let's not forget, thinking is our invisible doing.

Experts estimate that the mind thinks of 60,000- 80,000 thoughts every day. That is 2,500 –3,000 thoughts per hour or just under 50 thoughts per minute, and just under 1 per second. Even the esteemed neuroscientist and philosopher Dr. Deepak Chopra agrees. That is a lot of processing.

With processing so much information every day, for many of us, it feels as if we are on fast forward all the time. Our bodies and our minds need a break. We often feel the stress of this and we can easily experience feelings of anxiety, worry, and go into overwhelm. Then we wonder why we cannot fall asleep or get a good night's sleep. Consumer Reports surveys show that 68% or an estimated 164 Million Americans struggle with sleep. Americans spent 41 billion dollars on sleep aids and remedies in past years and that is expected to grow to 52 billion by 2020.

Moments are fleeting, hours go by, days become weeks, weeks turn into months and time keeps going and we still have our 'to do' lists. We update them, adding more items while crossing off others. When does it end? How do we catch up?

DO YOU THINK IT IS TIME TO INTERRUPT OUR THINKING?

Take a moment and think about your computer, iPad, tablet or phone. Look at the programs running constantly on your devices. Look at the number of files and websites open, and your increasing emails and text messages. There is a lot going on simultaneously. This can be overload for your device. At times, you need to simply close applications. You may need to save and file documents that are important and delete files that are no longer needed that just take up space. You need to check for viruses, scan and clean your computer. At some point, you need to back up what is important and delete emails, files, photos, and applications that are no longer needed.

We all need to refresh, restart, shut down and update our devices. We install new updates in order to have an efficiently-running system. When our computers freeze, we need to do an emergency control, alt, delete or simply shut down our operating systems. Daily maintenance is shutting off unnecessary programs and apps running so your devices can conserve energy and battery power.

We, as human beings, need to recharge our own systems, our health and energy reserves. We need to listen to our bodies. They are always talking to us. We often do not hear what our bodies are telling us. Perhaps we have the chills, feel low in energy, feel the onset of a cold or just feel off. We may feel lower back pain, have eye strain from looking at our computers or a stiff neck as we look down at our cell phones. We may have a low-grade headache, a low blood sugar, or low energy mid-afternoon that is telling us we need to eat, or just take a break. Our body is always talking to us. Do we hear it? Do we stop and address the signs? This is when we need to take time out, if only for moments, and this means it is time to interrupt what we are doing and how we are doing things.

We need to refresh our bodies, minds, and souls throughout the day. We need sleep to restore and allow healing.

- **How does this relate to your Life and how does this relate to your Space?**

Imagine a period of 15, 30, 45 or even 60 minutes in your day, where the distractions of everyday life fall away and you are calm and quiet. There are no computers, iPads, phones, TVs or radios, and no irritating sounds, personality conflicts or negative energies in your environment. Imagine there is no interference, traffic, pollution, construction sounds or distracting smells. There is no spouse, no children, no parents, no friends, no one. There is just you. This is your time to claim time for you.

> **Imagine that the *only* thing for you to do is To Be.**

Imagine having a 'To Be' List. How many of us have ever had one of these? . . . Exactly!

That is my point. To Be, how does one do that?

It is possible to simply allow your thoughts to come into your mind, notice them, acknowledge them, and then let them flow from you into the air. As we become more aware of our thoughts, we become more aware of our feelings. This helps us to release our thoughts. Stillness does influence us, allowing us to create more awareness and more space.

> **How does one release thoughts?**

Not unlike how we have an edit and delete button on our computers and devices, we, as human beings, can use any hobby or form of relaxation such as meditation to help us accomplish turning the volume of the outside and inside world down for ourselves. For example, relaxing with soft music and being in a quiet space. By closing our eyes and simply visualizing, we can create a space of calm and of quiet where we notice our thoughts, like a portal where thoughts flow in and out. We can simply notice and observe what thoughts come up. We can feel how our bodies respond. Our bodies may tense up or they may relax. The important thing is that we notice our thoughts and how they make us feel.

The first step is simply becoming aware of your thoughts. The second step is not having any judgement about them, but rather to notice and acknowledge them, giving them space and permission to be. Air is free, space is free... It is ok for them to just be. With having just under 50 thoughts per minute, we can allow many of those thoughts to just go, releasing themselves and floating from our consciousness. Our job is to simply notice our thoughts and give them freedom to be.

Thoughts are simply things, they just are. They have no meaning on their own. Meaning comes to them as a result of what we attach to them. The point is, that in doing this and by simply noticing your thoughts, you start to create space for yourself. This is the beginning of the process in creating space for you. Thoughts may stay with you. They may even become clearer to you or you may interpret them differently. They may create emotions and that is ok. There is no right or wrong, and there is no judgement to be had. Just let thoughts be.

> **Mind Massage Anyone?**

Taking time to meditate is a mind massage you give yourself. Anything that feels unlike home in your core, that does not resonate comfortably within you, can leave your body. When anything feels unlike love, your body's response system will simply give it permission to float away from your energy field into the universe.

There is nothing for you to decide. Your job is not to think, that is doing. Your job is to relax into your body, and into your heart, simply noticing your thoughts and let them be. Thoughts that are not serving you, i.e., chatter, noise, the thoughts that weigh you down, you don't need them. You can simply let them go. Did you know that you get to have a say about those thoughts? You can release them from your mind, freeing yourself up, so you create more space for you. With advanced techniques, you will learn how to quieten the mind chatter as easily as you delete files in your computer.

➢ **Do you want more space, more time, and more freedom in your life?**

Do what makes you comfortable and just relax. You may have more than one way to relax, the more the better. With consistent practice and making this a daily process, you will find that, over time, your mind will begin to quieten.

You will come to feel what is just the right amount of stillness for you. You will feel the soothing of your soul and that calm place inside that is just right for you. When you resonate with your internal rhythm and your breathing, you will have fleeting moments of that place where **Stillness Will Speak to you**. It will be divine.

When truly in a quiet place, it is then when you allow your mind to be still, and when everything else disappears. Just breathe. This will be an ah ha moment for you!

Imagine yourself in the perfect physical space that is comfortable and just right for you. There are no interruptions in this place. This space is your safe place. You can have the colors around you that you like, and the temperature that is just right for you. You may imagine yourself to be in an outdoor space such as nature, in your back yard, your garden in the mountains or your favorite vacation spot. Perhaps you are getting a massage, or maybe you are listening to your favorite music. Maybe you are playing an instrument or enjoying a hobby that nurtures you. Whatever relaxes you, that is where you need to be. This is your perfect space for you. This is where you get to create more and more space for you.

When we are most comfortable within ourselves, and in our quiet relaxed space inside, this is when stillness speaks to us, and magic can happen in our lives. We can feel elated, blissful, things occur effortlessly, time stands still, and there is an ease in our lives in those moments. Do you ever wonder why sometimes things just fall into place and everything runs smoothly? That is what I'm talking about. These moments and times are too few for most people.

➢ **How do I get more of these moments?**

In Stillness, our inner voice and our wisdom speaks. When we are consumed with thoughts and doing all the time, . . . there is no space for us to hear. That is why, when we invite more calm and peace into our lives, we can expand our space.

> ➤ **How do we expand our space?**

You need to be available for yourself on all levels and allow yourself to connect with your inner core. Allowing stillness to speak to you is not about finding more time, it's about how you perceive time and thus create more time. It is about valuing you.

> ➤ **How do I get to the point WHERE STILLNESS SPEAKS to me?**

You schedule work, fitness, meals and appointments into your day, now it is time to schedule you in your life. Now is the time for you to be your Number One Priority. This should be your most important goal.

Step 1. Meditate. Make the commitment of creating time every day, and find a hobby, activity, or an interest you enjoy, (a sport, gardening, cooking, bike riding, music or drawing, these are all forms of meditations), to help you relax.

Step 2. Be Mindful to claim this time and space for you alone. It is not to be shared with others.

Step 3. Decide on dedicated time(s) of day and an amount of time between 20 and 60 minutes each day to be in your space. (20-60 minutes, i.e., 1- 4 times a day). Inform others you are not to be interrupted under any circumstances. One of the best times to do this is the first hour of your morning, in what some of the most successful people develop into a habit they call their "Power Hour."

Step 4. Choose a method to induce relaxation and a meditative state. Visit: www.havingalifeofmore.com for materials and meditations to support your spiritual growth.

Step 5. Allow your thoughts to come to you freely. Simply notice them without judgment giving them freedom to be and have a voice. (This takes time.)

Step 6. Ask your inner self to speak to you and ask what messages it has for you.

Step 7. Keep Expanding your space and know that in this expansion the silence will speak to you longer and with more clarity.

Step 8. Journal every day. Having your own Personal Mindful and Gratitude Journal to write down your simple everyday observations ever so small, will be extraordinary for you.

You can meditate anywhere because your imagination can take you anywhere. The important thing is to establish a consistent time for you each day. Remember air is free and the space you create for yourself is free. It will add so much healing and quality to your life, you will be amazed.

For free techniques, meditations, journaling pages, and more, please go to: www.havingalifeofmore.com where you can share your story with us on what works for you and how your STILLNESS SPEAKS to you. Please share this with your family and friends. More information, transformational workshops, online programs, retreats and more, can be found at: www.havingalifeofmore.com.

Your internal GPS (internal navigational system/life compass) comes alive when you Connect with it. It is up to you to Connect with it. This is the gift of kindness you give to yourself. You are truly in your space when there is nothing else. This is when STILLNESS SPEAKS.

Indulge and experience the Stillness Within You. *You can ask for guidance and direction and you can ENRICH your life every day.*

About Cheryl

Cheryl Ivaniski, D.Ac., C.H., RDH is a Health Authority and Lifestyle Wellness Strategist. She inspires, empowers and educates people in a way that heightens their awareness to live their best quality of life.

Cheryl is an Award-Winning Author, Wellness Coach, Mentor and Advocate who teaches you how to live your best life vibrantly well. She is the Co-Author of *Success Starts Today* with Jack Canfield, International and *New York Times* Best-Selling Author.

Cheryl earned her Doctorate in Holistic Studies in Traditional Chinese Medicine and Acupuncture, her Certification in Holistic Nutrition and Kinesiology, and is a Certified Hypnotherapist and NLP practitioner. Cheryl began her career as a Registered Dental Hygienist in private practice, and teaching as a College Professor. She authored 30 Modules of Education becoming a Consultant and Mentor training Doctors, teams of professionals and Keynote Speaking Nationwide. She believes in combining Traditional and Naturopathic practices for an Integrative Approach to Wellness while embracing a Spiritual connection to nourish our body, mind and soul. She believes this is when true healing occurs.

Cheryl's appetite 'for more' expanded to immune system wellness as a result of her unexpected diagnosis of Type I Diabetes and Thyroid disease (Hashimoto's disease) simultaneously. With her passion, education, and life experience, she began her private practice in Toronto, Ontario in 1997 and founded the Diabetes Wellness Centre creating the (HDEP) Holistic Diabetes Educators Program. With its ongoing development, Cheryl has authored over 50 modules of education offering Doctors, professionals, and caregivers advanced training, while individual and family programs help people to neutralize blood sugar levels, reverse diabetes, and help prevent complications. Cheryl truly understands what it is like to live with these challenges every day, just like hundreds of millions of people around the world who are pre-diabetic and are at risk, or who have diabetes and immune system challenges.

Cheryl's newest award-winning Inspirational Book, *Having A Life of More*, walks you step-by-step through the 10 Wellness Principles that teach you how to have "Your Life of More." She shares the life lessons her Grandparents taught her - who lived well into their 90's. In upcoming Special Presentations, Cheryl shares "The Special Secrets to Living Healthy at 100 years young" that her Grandfather instilled in her.

Cheryl continues her coaching with world-renowned spiritual and business coaches. She is a self-made accredited real estate investor, entrepreneur, and CEO of multiple businesses.

In Cheryl's "Life of More," she enjoys country music, walks in nature, meditation, gourmet cooking, travelling, interior design, renovating, piano playing and volleyball.

Cheryl has written feature articles in journals, been a guest on nationally-syndicated television and radio shows, a keynote speaker for Businesses, Associations, Foundations, Training Facilities and Special Interest Groups.

Cheryl wants to *help* you reach people globally and is now Accepting Special Assignments for television, radio, and media interviews. To invite Cheryl to host, commentate and/or be a keynote speaker for your upcoming event, and to learn about her programs, seminars and retreats, please visit:

- www.havingalifeofmore.com
- www.diabeteswellnesscentre.com

Please feel free to call: 1-877-255-1953.

CHAPTER 17

SUCCESS *IS* TO FEEL HAPPY TODAY

BY DR. CONNY BLUNT

A Simple Guide to Smart Living for the 21st Century

A decade ago, my life appeared to be over. I remember waking up to what seemed a cake on fire next to the bed and excited whispers breaking into the ritual 'Happy Birthday' song. Before welcoming my family with a big smile, I hid my head under the pillow and watched my life pass before my eyes in a moment. It's been an amazing life.

My wildest dreams have come true. And I used to dream big – despite growing up in East Berlin during the Cold War, where I was conditioned from an early age not to expect much. I enjoyed a pretty 'ordinary' childhood. My loving parents were full of flaws. My youth was interesting. I trained amongst the top gymnasts in East Germany (nearly making it to the 1980 Moscow Olympics).

Then in 1986, I escaped from the communist East to the West – before the Berlin Wall came down. It was a dream that I'd had for years, but realising it was considered impossible by most people on either side of The Wall. But I did succeed against the odds, and as a result my 20s were wild, and life was an endless party. I relished my freedom and travelled to exotic countries. Every day was an adventure.

By comparison, in my 30s I did all the *'grown-up'* things. I wanted to settle down. I found love. I became a wife and then a mother. I had an idyllic home – even a garden with wild passion flowers growing everywhere – and I forged a successful career in medicine as an anaesthetist.

I thought: "I have made it! I am healthy and have absolutely everything I could wish for."

But then, horrified, I continued in my thoughts, "This doesn't feel even close to the way I had imagined it would. I no longer feel happy. I am so tired. My successes feel empty. I feel dazed, drained, tense, bored, irritable, burnt out, numb and desperately lonely – despite my lovely family standing next to me."

I pulled myself together, sat up straight, filled my lungs like mighty bellows and extinguished all 41 candles at once. In the split second of darkness and absolute silence that followed, I found myself questioning everything, *"What has happened to me and how? What am I missing?"*

Perhaps you've asked yourself those same questions? This is, after all, a rampant First World dilemma. It was only when I took a break from my busy life, jumped off the racing treadmill, stood absolutely still for a while and faced up to the compromises I'd made and the dreams I'd abandoned, that the fog began to clear.

I reflected on the reasons for my 'empty success':

- I realised I'd stopped being fearlessly authentic
- I no longer trusted in my own instinct
- I was no longer in tune with my true nature

Cutting myself off from my true nature meant that I literally could no longer feel myself. I'd lost my inner balance. Instead of following my heart, my gut instincts, my intuition and responding appropriately to the obvious natural warning signs, I had allowed logic and rational thinking to obscure my heart's desires.

(THINKING... it's one of the things that make us human but it's also a process that can disconnect us from reality. It's been suggested that all thinking is over-thinking.)

I tried so hard to conform to the life that society expected of me and I was slowly dying in the process. How did I get out of this mess?

Simply, I learned to relax – I mean deliberately, courageously and consciously relax – like I have never knowingly relaxed before in my entire life. It's how you begin to reset your physiology into balance. Scientific studies have confirmed that happiness and success occur when you achieve your **Natural State of Physiological Balance.**

It was a turning point. When I thought I'd done it all, lived it all, experienced it all (a splendid example of over-thinking), little did I suspect that the best part of my life was only just about to begin, bringing experiences that eclipsed everything I'd lived up to before.

Over the decade that followed – a decade of worldwide travel, study, practice, experiments and experiences, I became an expert in the art of 'how to actively relax', how to capitalise on the extraordinary rewards to be had from relaxing - and how to teach it.

I discovered that to be in control of 'being out of control' is a supreme skill that will transform your life. It's like jumping out of a perfectly safe aeroplane, able to admire the beautiful view as you fly, with absolute certainty that your parachute will open and get you safely back to earth.

Or, on a more practical note, true relaxation means you can remain calm, receptive, sensitive, logical, creative and happy – even when challenged by life, be it in a highly demanding or high-risk job, delivering a speech to thousands of people, defusing an argument at home, dealing with an illness, or expressing your desires openly and courageously.

When you learn to slow down, stop and be perfectly still that's when all the good things start to happen! The present moment …

- Connects you to your happy nature
- Energises you every day
- Resets your physiology to health, harmony and balance
- Gives you plenty of pointers and assists to decide your next moves in life
- Can renew your life, your relationships and shift your team dynamics positively
- Opens doors on new perspectives, limitless possibilities and exciting choices

- Propels you beyond your current horizon where an infinite view of your future awaits you

The present moment holds HUGE potentials wherein you can regain your momentum towards creating the life you *really* want to live. You know... the one you daren't think about because it feels impossibly out of reach right now.

It's about living LIFE ON YOUR TERMS. Today I have embedded this powerful notion into my life; a life guided by **The Holistic Life System**.

This is a **scalable formula** that:

— Consists of small, effective steps that promote the power and benefits of natural living in the 21st century
— Results in genuine happiness every day, leading to meaningful success
— Works with new paradigms, advanced technologies and new ways of thinking, feeling and living

Let me show you how you can begin to integrate this simple formula into your everyday life.

INTRODUCING THE HOLISTIC LIFE SYSTEM
If you want to be happy and successful you need to be 'energy aware'.

The **Holistic Life System** is a natural lifestyle programme, designed to sharpen your Energy Awareness.

But why is that important?

Energy... it may sound like a kind of magic, but it's really just about systematically tapping into vital information that is inherent in your powerful nature.

You may not be able to touch, see or hear energy, but energy is still there. You may not be aware of energy at all .... or maybe you call it something else, such as your emotional intelligence, your intuition, a sixth sense, or your soul. Depending on your culture you might recognise it described as Chi, Chakras and Kundalini. Energy is 'a knowing' that every human being can access. And Energy Awareness can provide you, at a profound level, with insights into what you should be doing now (and next) to create a life that has meaning for you.

That's why Energy Awareness is at the core of our teachings and the backbone of The Holistic Life System. Take a look at the following equation…

The Holistic Life System

Your Natural Brilliance = **Your Essential Energy**
[Happiness + Success]   [Feel It + Imagine It + Live It]

The reason this system works is because it focuses on the very essence of your existence, which *IS*, in fact, energy.

It's now common knowledge (that's confirmed by hard and irrefutable scientific evidence) that you are $E=mc^2$.

You are energy in motion – E-MOTION in a constant flux. You can feel it as your Essential Energy.

And if you want to create meaningful change and enjoy happiness every day, then this is where you need to look. You'd see this truth with your own eyes if you were to look at yourself under a subatomic microscope. As the microscope zooms into your microcosm – past the cells, molecules and atoms to the particle or quantum level – you'd see that you are in fact the sum total of seven billion, billion, billion quanta.

What's remarkable about quanta is they can behave as both wave and particle at the same time.

This means you are both a physical body and an energy body, SIMULTANEOUSLY. This means that whilst your physical being is rooted in time and space, your energy can be anywhere and everywhere, because this is how your quanta behave.

Your quanta can communicate their configuration over distances from the tip of your nose to the edge of the universe outside of space-time:

- They can disappear on one side of a classically 'insurmountable' energy barrier and reappear on the other side more energised.

- They choose the state they take depending on your intentions.

- They carry all the information there is about you (each quantum can hold up to several megabits of information).

- And they have memory – your memory.

In other words, thanks to your quanta, you have the intelligence and the reach of a biological internet.

What's more, everything you experience as reality – the world around you and your own body – is actually made up of 99.999999% space. This space is filled with vacuum energy, a latent form of energy that modern physicists calculate to be 110 orders of magnitude greater than the radiant energy at the centre of the sun. Imagine that!

The significant point here is that instead of exclusively paying attention to your physical world, we want you to focus your attention on the energy that actually defines it.

What's more, you will discover that reality is the best sensation there is...

That's why at Ki2Energi we're dedicated to revealing the knowledge and the techniques that are known to deepen your Energy Awareness.

Let us show you how to put all this energy talk into practice.

THREE STEPS TO HAPPINESS AND HARMONY EVERY DAY

At Ki2Energi we teach Energy Awareness in three steps...

Step 1 – Feel It!
Feel Your Energy! Energy Awareness and Happiness

To introduce people to the process of becoming energy aware, I refer to what I call Energy Clues. These 'clues' occur spontaneously at the height of any human experience and provide you with a glimpse of your Essential Energy. In other words, Energy Clues are clues (and in many cases a reminder) of how good life can feel for YOU.

We've all had them. They're the moments when you feel elated and ecstatic, content and connected, joyful, in awe and brimming with a love of life. Maybe a first kiss or achieving a long sought-after goal, lying under a carpet of a million stars, or gazing into your newborn's eyes…

These moments are important because **they're your point of reference for how success and happiness FEELS FOR YOU**. It's how life should feel for you – *EVERY DAY!* Consequently, your Energy Clues are the benchmark that help you gauge whether or not you're making the right choice at any given moment.

During our workshops, we'll share techniques with you that will increasingly enable you to revive your Energy Clues with such an intensity that they feel as if they're occurring right now.

<u>Step 2 – Imagine It!</u>
Imagine Your Energy! Energy Awareness and Eureka

Not only do Energy Clues show you how good life can feel, they also contain eureka moments… those moments of genius insight that seem to come from nowhere. And these are key pieces of information that assist you in creating an inspired existence.

Contrary to popular belief, eureka moments aren't the exclusive preserve of saints or geniuses. In fact, *these insights are available to us all.*

They occur when you're in a physiological state of relaxation, balance and wellbeing. Remember Archimedes, who was sitting in the bath when he had that original eureka moment! They happen when your physiology is most coherent and your potential for optimised biological (including mental) efficiency and performance is at its greatest. Such profound experiences are less likely to occur when you're stressed, anxious, unhappy, agitated, hyperactive, chasing deadlines or in pain.

Let me explain how it works...

When your energy physiology is incoherent, your body is like an incandescent light bulb that can still light up a room but because the light is radiated at so many different frequencies, a large proportion of the energy is 'wasted' and dissipates as heat. In practical terms, this is the equivalent of feeling disorganized and scatter-brained.

By comparison, when your energy is coherent, you function like a laser beam; the same amount of energy has the potential to reach the surface of a distant planet.

When your energy is coherent, you are in sync with the world and feel that you can do anything! You feel physically invigorated and exceptionally happy – you are in a completely optimised biological state. That's when you have inspired ideas triggered by your natural sense of happiness, rather than by external stimuli or ulterior motives that have nothing to do with you.

Your eureka moments are powerful indicators designed to help you make the right choices. They generate:

- New and even genius ideas
- An explosion of your creativity and imagination
- Discovery of solutions that are perfect for your situation
- Total clarity for your next move
- A clear vision of exactly what it is that makes you happy
- An exceptional life each and every day and a brilliant future

In our workshops, you'll discover plenty of techniques that can help make eureka moments a daily occurrence.

Step 3 – Live It!
Enjoy the Benefits! Energy Awareness and Results

The final piece of the jigsaw is simple - yet crucial.

While it's well known that FEELING happy and IMAGINING a happy future – and that includes imagining clear action steps - accounts for around 80% of your success, your success is not complete until you actually take action. We'll show you techniques designed to help you activate your Essential Energy - experience your Energy Clues and eureka moments – and create an impetus that brings real results.

Let's have a quick recap ...

In this chapter, I've shared some powerful, introductory ideas about the link between energy and your everyday happiness that lead to meaningful success.

This is the point at which the science of the physical and the metaphysical world and the human experience of the physical and metaphysical overlap. This is the missing link between your logical analytical brain and your intuitive heart. This is an opportunity to connect deeply with your powerful innate nature and to access the insights and resources necessary to create the life of your dreams – but in the real world.

Happiness is Physiology in Balance
High on Energy – High on Life – Harmony Every Day

About Dr. Conny Blunt

Conny Blunt is a medical doctor in the UK and the founder and CEO of Ki2energi.

She believes happiness and success are natural states of our physiology in balance and harmony; a default setting that can be lived by us all - all the time. And it's from this state that you can create a life you love.

This is regardless of how lacking your childhood or how challenging your current situation. In fact, Conny's own life is such an example.

Growing up in East Berlin during the Cold War, Conny lived an unconventional life in a deeply communist state. As a child, she trained amongst the top gymnasts (nearly making it to the Moscow Olympics), but in her teens the love for freedom became her greatest passion.

This instinct and desire led her to take great risk in escaping from East to West Germany in 1986 - before the Berlin Wall came down. Capitalizing on her newfound opportunities, Conny lived and worked in five different countries while forging a career in medicine as a consultant anaesthetist.

Initially, Conny followed her intuition – inspired by the boundless possibilities of life, she gravitated towards experiences that brought happiness and success. Over the last decade she has systematically dedicated her work and worldwide studies to make what she intuitively discovered more easily accessible to all. It's become her mission to create a system for smart living in the 21st century by developing practical applications that integrate modern sciences and Eastern traditions.

That's because the subject that gets her most fired up is energy awareness - a skill that naturally resets our physiology to balance and harmony. It is the key skill of our times because it allows us to fully explore, grasp, and experience the splendour of our human existence.

In this book, Conny Blunt highlights that the scientific definition of energy that's evolved since Einstein ($E = mc^2$) and the subtle energies postulated by ancient cultures are simply two world views of the same extraordinary reality that we inhabit. It is a reality that's waiting to be noticed by each and every one of us.

That's because it is by becoming energy aware that we can tap into our powerful innate nature, gain insights, and access the resources that are necessary to create the life of our dreams – in the real world.

On a personal level, passion is what makes every minute of her life count. A life that is guided by The Holistic Life System - a scalable formula that she has developed in collaboration with her Ki2energi team. This system puts energy awareness up to the top in the must-know curriculum of the modern WoMan. Integrating essential teachings, philosophies, and practices from masters in their field in the East and the West, it provides simple, practical steps that can make exceptional health, happiness, and success a tangible experience every day for everybody.

CHAPTER 18

360 DEGREES OF SUCCESS

BY DR. BRAD GLOWAKI ("DR. GLOW")

The most important work we can do in the world begins with ourselves. In fact, before we can truly invest in helping others, we need to invest in ourselves first. We don't always realize how our mind, what we eat, and how we treat our body can impact our overall outlook on life. However, the truth is that it does.

With this perspective in mind, it is important to remember that we are all connected in numerous ways and, in turn, our actions can ultimately affect – whether negative or positive – the lives of others. This puts emphasis on our personal health not only as a factor in our own bodies, but also one that impacts those connected to us, as well.

It is important that each of us learn to look at life through a holistic lens. This means making intentional, well-rounded choices that allow us to live a life with 360 degrees of success. One step towards this way of thinking is understanding that a healthy body and mind will dramatically change your life for the better.

In thinking about your health in 360 degrees, you are empowered to:

1. Identify and make the necessary changes in your life for the better
2. Uncover ways to apply healthy living to all aspects of your life
3. Achieve success

In the process, you might be surprised to find that not all our solutions are wrapped up in modern medicine. In fact, a staggering number of people are relying on prescription and over-the-counter solutions for ailments their own bodies are capable of correcting naturally! Additionally, it's important to recognize that not everyone that the media presents as an ambassador of health and wellness actually is an accurate representation of best practices.

In this chapter, I hope to touch on a few easy areas you can influence a healthier lifestyle, and make changes towards living your life in 360 degrees success so that you can positively influence your life and, in turn, those of others connected to you.

----- oOo -----

DR. GLOW

My journey towards becoming a doctor started after a fateful accident that changed my path in ways I couldn't have anticipated. When I was 16, I fractured my arm while playing sports in high school and was told I wouldn't be able to use it ever again. I was young enough to feel like I had my whole life in front of me, and as an athlete, you can imagine this was the worst news I could have received. However, life has a way of working out for you in the end.

At the time, I was determined to gain the full functionality of my arm again, which is what started me on my path to researching different resources for a cure. Since I refused to accept what I was receiving in terms of care and support, I went out seeking alternative methods and treatment. What I learned set me on my own personal health journey. During this time, I also discovered that I not only loved learning about the body, but I also loved teaching.

I should mention that I never had to give up on my desire to become an athlete. I became an All-American & Division I Lacrosse player in college, and even received a scholarship to play. Not bad for a kid who was told he would be sidelined permanently.

It was because of this personal hardship and potential handicap that I discovered my passion. Ironically, I found so much relief while still being in the cast from this injury, because through this process I found my career path at just 16 years old. I wanted to be a chiropractor! After college, I attended chiropractic school, and post-graduation, opened my own private practice in Seal Beach, CA at age 25. As a former athlete, I started attracting professional athletes as patients. From the beginning, I've focused on a holistic approach to health and wellness, and built my practice on the firm foundational belief that your physical, nutritional, and mental health all are key components of a successful, balanced life.

My goal is to teach people how to best implement healthy strategies into their day to day lives. Often this means looking at what many consider "alternative" remedies, but are actually natural solutions compared to synthetic medications. It also means providing a common sense framework to help people make healthier, well-rounded choices enabling them to live out their dreams of being truly accomplished and genuinely happy – living a life with 360 degrees of success. The more engaged you are in your own health, the better healthcare you will receive.

The significant accomplishments I've achieved in my private practice generated a demand from others around the world to learn the "secrets" to my success. This global interest is what led to the creation of the Wellness Champions. Presently, I also provide trainings, as well as organize special events as a wellness expert, to teach other wellness advocates all over the world how to spread that same vital message in their local communities. I'm delighted to recognize all of the doctors who are a part of this organization, all who support and teach people about true health. In some cases we view these teachings as influencing healthy changes in workplaces and schools. Most often people take what they have learned and make transformations in their homes and private lives that set them up for success in ways they couldn't have imagined before. My goal is to positively impact the lives of millions to achieve what I proudly refer to as: 360 degrees of success.

WELLNESS PARADIGM: 360 DEGREES OF SUCCESS

I want to kick-off this section by declaring that I strongly believe that everyone is capable of achieving 360 degrees of success for themselves.

To live a life with 360 degrees of success, you need to embark on this journey by entering into a specific mindset. You need to acknowledge that you are a performer as well as a high achiever. You might define a performer as someone who needs to carry out a specific role. However, this doesn't always look just one way. These days, most of us lead rich and multi-faceted lives, executing multiple roles in our day to day. Therefore, all of us are performers in a myriad of ways.

So what does an all-star athlete, an ambitious CEO of a tech startup, and an artist and mother-of-three all have in common? They are all performers who need to maximize their rhythms and rituals to be a tool of their 360 degrees of success.

Your rhythms and rituals ultimately determine how effective you are in your daily life and ultimately how well you perform in your multiple roles. Performance can be measured on a wellness paradigm of 360 degrees.

We should begin by talking about Hippocrates well-known saying: "Let food be thy medicine." In this context, food can be the healing sauce, but it can also be the poison if we're not careful. I believe these things are the foundation that leads to a person's success as a performer, regardless of the role they have.

Rhythms, in essence, are cycles in the body that need to function at an optimal level. For example, sleep cycles: they last 90 minutes, and it is recommended that we each go through five cycles each night. (Other examples of cycles are menstrual cycles and digestion cycles.) On the other hand, rituals are what we call the habits we form in our daily lives that vary greatly from person to person. Workout routines, how and when we eat and how often we hydrate are all prime examples of rituals.

Studying the lives and habits of highly-effective people, we see some patterns. What's important to note in many cases is that these people vary greatly by age, ability, background, profession, and life choices. Despite this, after observing these people, we can gather that they have a few key things in common. They have established rhythms and rituals which are optimal and lead to their success as performers. For example, restful sleep, healthy diets, and active minds with permission for rest and leisure. In other words, these people do well in life because they are alert, well rested and nourished.

Closely observe your rhythm and rituals. Draw two columns on a piece of paper: one of the things you believe you are doing well to take care of yourself (e.g., going for a daily walk, eating a variety of vegetables, etc.), and another of things that need improvement (e.g., eating dinner too late, drinking enough water, etc.). Chances are, you already have a few ideas of healthy changes you can make to be more effective. Come back to this list every week as an accountability check, and look to make changes as needed.

Additionally, don't think of energy as a limited resource, like an hourglass. To be able to be successful in different areas of life (in 360 degrees of success), one must allow each need to demand the resources it deserves. In this case, a mentally-demanding job should not take away from the energy it takes to plan a surprise birthday party for a spouse. Conversely, the energy it takes to get your kids ready for school should not take away from the energy it takes to be a good friend. Treat each facet of your rich life with the care and nourishment it requires. Pay attention to the demands of the day and always remember to be intentional with your resources. This will allow you to be successful as a performer in your varying day-to-day roles.

One should also note that your mindset is a very important factor that leads to your success as a performer. The brain is responsible for many functions, and in successful people, we look a lot at how the brain records and predicts information. When the brain functions as a recorder of the past, it is setting you on a path for similar future experiences. This is in part because your brain is a predictor of the future, based on your history.

In other words, you repeat doing what you did in the past because of your limited thinking. Therefore, your future outcomes are not enhanced. This is all part of another cycle, a ritual and rhythm. The way you think leads to the way you act, and the way you act leads to specific results... and the cycle then repeats. Keep this in mind, as you identify your rhythms and rituals, be sure to elevate your mental acuity to create better actions which will create better results – catapulting you closer to living a life with 360 degrees of success. Elevate your mindset! Dare to dream big. It's the only way to create everyday actions to get there! Your brain must be seeing things as you will be, to achieve balance and success.

As we all know, rest is extremely important for the brain and the body. Maximize what you are capable of accomplishing during waking hours by prioritizing quality sleep. Follow these helpful tips to make modifications and improve your quality of rest:

1. If you find yourself frequently fatigued, take time to analyze your eating and drinking habits, including the consumption of alcohol and stimulants like coffee.
2. Watch the heavy carbohydrates. While they may help you fall asleep, these foods are not good for staying asleep, which ultimately can lead to insomnia.
3. Practice "no screen time" at least one hour before bedtime. Another option is to use a red tinted light on your screen devices. This red tint (available on some cell phones and tablets) is a different LED frequency, proven to help relax and prevent over-stimulation of your eyes and brain.
4. Too much physical activity will wake up your brain, causing a cycle of fatigue if rest cannot be accomplished. While 'working out' can do wonders for your physique – building muscle, stamina, and improving your mood – it's important to limit workout time to hours during the day, and never later than 8:00 pm. In this sense, it's more ideal to get a good night's sleep than a late evening run: the proper rest will make you stronger and more effective.

THE INFORMATION SUPERHIGHWAY

Finally, living in the information age has impacted every aspect of our lives, including what we know about health and nutrition. However, with so many avenues to check out, it's hard to know what advice to take.

While it is important to pay attention to diet, rest, and exercise, it's also key to allow the work of professionals to support you. As a chiropractor, I know how important the work we do has been for patients – and not just for pain mitigation or release. You may not realize that your nervous system holds many important keys to your holistic health, including the control of the functions of the body. A spinal subluxation interrupts proper nerve flow, often without pain. This is why I highly recommend a central nervous system "tune up" for your body through regular chiropractic care if it is not already a part of your rhythms and rituals.

Like a car or any complex machine, it's critical to let a professional do a diagnosis on your key systems, and help make regular adjustments to keep everything running smoothly and get you that much closer to living a life with 360 degrees of success. Unlike a car, your body is not a machine. It is vitalistic and you can't trade this one in for a newer model.

What may surprise you a lot is how many of our existing beliefs about nutrition come from out-of-date information and even from corporations selling their agenda through synthetic medications. As mentioned earlier in the Chapter, you'd be surprised how many that are the "face" of health in the media are actually not. What's astonishing is the regularity with which misinformation is being spread, even within the healthcare community. Many of these sources do not want the simple truth out: that our bodies are capable of solving complex problems and healing ourselves naturally. A healthy lifestyle is an inside-out approach, not a medication shortage.

A HEALTHY WHOLE CAN CHANGE YOUR LIFE

In this chapter, you've learned a little bit about how healthy changes can start to impact your life in a positive way. It's important to start small and work in incremental ways and introduce more difficult changes once you have a regularity with your new routine.

Applying these simple principles to your life can improve your quality of life in tangible and immediate ways. When we look at our health from a 360-degree vantage point, we see just how interconnected our bodies are with our brains, heart, and stamina. We also understand just how much influence we have over our lives by making healthy choices and improving our attitudes.

Think of your health as a 3-legged stool. One leg represents physical health, one represents nutritional health, and one represents your mental health. If the stool wobbled, you'd flip it over to see which leg might need an adjustment. Conversely, if you ignored the problem, you just might find yourself swiftly on the floor with a bruised tailbone. This analogy reminds us to prioritize the holistic health of all three legs: our body, our nutrition, and our brains. When you strive for performance and accomplishment, you will need a strong foundation to prevail. Make sure your health habits are serving you well, and don't be afraid to analyze and make changes. Ultimately, it's up to you to prioritize a balanced lifestyle to live life to the fullest: in stereoscopic 360 degrees.

About Dr. Brad Glowaki ("Dr. Glow")

Teaching the world how to live a healthier lifestyle and defining what true health is has been Dr. Brad Glowaki's (Dr. Glow's) mission for the past 20 years.

He is a graduate of the University of Delaware and the Los Angeles College of Chiropractic. After chiropractic school, he went on to open his own private practice in the gorgeous beach town of Seal Beach, CA. He has been providing the local community, including elite and professional athletes, with holistic care for the last 20 years. Most recently, in 2012, he was at the London Olympics caring for his athletes on Team USA. In 2010, with 12,000 chiropractors in California, he was recognized as "Chiropractor of the Year."

Aside from being a chiropractor in private practice, he is a renowned international wellness speaker and educator. He is often out of the country sharing his results for health and wellness internationally. He speaks on four continents annually. Of notable mention, he has shared the stage with some of the top pioneers in healthcare, including most recently, Dr. Bennet Omalu – the inspiration for the hit-movie, *Concussion.*

When he is not speaking or in his practice, you can find him identifying different ways to spread the message of health and wellness far and wide. One of the ways he has done that is through founding the Wellness Champions, a non-profit organization comprised of wellness experts throughout the world looking to promote health and wellness in their communities. To date, there are wellness experts that are a part of this organization on six continents.

Dr. Brad Glowaki has been consistently recognized as a leading chiropractor in the field. Most recently, he has been recognized as one of the top ten chiropractors making a global impact in chiropractic and healthcare. Prior to this, he was the 2012 Parker Seminar's "Chiropractor of the Year" and in 2005 he was voted to the National Register's "Who's Who?" list of top chiropractors nationwide.

Of all his accomplishments, he is most proud of being a father to four outstanding children – Georgia, Luke, Saylor, and Hero – and husband to his beautiful and supportive wife, Jessica.

To learn more about the Wellness Champions or to inquire about having a wellness expert go to your organization or workplace to share a healthy message, please visit:
- www.wellnesschampions.org

CHAPTER 19

PERSISTENCE

BY DR. JONATHAN AGBEBIYI

Many roads lead to Rome, as the proverbial statement goes, and each one of us finds his or her Rome, and decides on what road to where one wants to go. Understandably, many of us know that there are many obstacles obstructing getting from point A to point B, on the way to achieving any goal, regardless of how simple the goal seems. Remember how difficult your first bicycle ride? The thoughts regarding staying on the bike, balance, fear of falling, of getting bruised? But then, after wiggling and wobbling, you stayed on the bike for the first time and went for a while before falling. You got back on the bike again, practiced until you got so good that you protested and your parents had to peel you off your bike. Here, your persistence paid off. It became fun and enjoyment after the fact.

Great! How about swimming? The same experience; and before that, it was the same with crawling, hanging and pulling yourself up the chair or table or whatever was available to help you stand up. Then you took baby steps. It was challenging, and nobody could keep up with you when you finally learnt to walk. That was innate persistence. The awkwardness of the traditional way of holding a violin did not keep you from learning it, even though your fingers and wrist hurt. You persevered and were glad when you achieved proficiency to play to everyone's delight. This is stick-to-it-ive-ness perseverance.

It is true and thank goodness that you were young then, and did not create obstructions to success for yourself. As we grow, events and circumstances become issues and issues manifest as obstructions, which become the challenges and obstacles on the way to achieving our goals. Lots of these obstacles are self-created challenges and real obstructions, unforeseen or fathomed. These test and challenge us to prove ourselves equal and worthy of the destination, the fleece or the grail we set out after, which by perseverance and persistence we emerge, even though bruised, but changed, stronger and wiser.

All of us have what it takes because we are born that way, judging from our earlier achievements. Regardless of the outlook, the deformities or physical impediments which cause us to whimper and ask, "How can anyone do that?" we wonder in amazement at how successful some people are, regardless of their condition, deformities and challenges; how they transcend these obstacles to emerge, teaching the rest of us the powers of the human spirit and what it can accomplish with determination and perseverance.

Challenges keep many people from reaching their goals, but with persistence and perseverance come success and achievement of dreams. Kentucky Fried Chicken™ pioneer, Colonel Sanders, did not let age prevent him from reaching his goals. He achieved his goals in his 60's, after enduring a brutal stepfather and the hardship of farm work in his earlier years. Senator John Glenn went into space for the second time at age 77; he, too, transcended the age limitation.

Unable to transcend and persevere, some blame deformities, heredity, genetic defects, war injuries or accidents for their lack of achievement. And still, hereditary deformities, either through birth trauma or genetically inherited, does not stop many in achieving their goals regardless of the hardships. There are many others who also suffered the same fate during the war, and came about great achievements, as is the case of Daniel Inouye, for whom the loss of his right hand during his leadership in the war shelved his dream of becoming a surgeon, and instead, neither lead a pity party nor remained complacent, but went on, schooled himself in politics, and achieved greatness as a statesman for the state of Hawaii (in both Congress and the Senate).

Many use lack of money as a complaint preventing their success. I submit to you that some of the world's billionaires raised themselves from poverty in the streets and achieved financial success, having labored and persistently persevered.

Despite mounting evidence that it's becoming increasingly difficult to build such wealth, there are incredible stories which are proof that it is possible to overcome life's daunting and toughest challenges with persistence, creating better outcomes. Guy Laliberté started as a hired hand in the circus and became the CEO of *Cirque du Soleil*, with a worth of about $2.7 billion. Ms. Ursula Burns was raised by her single parent, poor, in a housing project and still became the first African-American woman CEO to head a Fortune 500 Company, Xerox. Kerkorian learned English on the streets, had little education and was a casualty of the Great Depression with his family; he persisted to become successful with his net worth stated to be about $17 billion dollars.

Frederick Douglas desired education and was determined to succeed when it was illegal for slaves to be educated, denying them the knowledge to free themselves. He persevered and suffered the slave master's many lashes and beatings and the separation of his family. He endured and secretly taught himself – after which he taught other slaves, empowered himself, and joined other abolitionists, many of whom were effective in helping to free other slaves.

Who knew of Famous Amos, an older African-American at the time, who nurtured his dream of wonderful tasty cookies. He even pursued it while Betty Croker was queen of cookies? Nobody knew him, until now. 'Famous Amos' is now a famous name regardless of his ethnicity. The Williams sisters pursued their dreams and achieved success, regardless of their sex, ethnicity, financial status or education.

You could be just as determined, persevere and be as persistent as Muhammad Ali who was stripped of his title because of his religion – changing from Christianity to Muhammadanism. Incarcerated for years because of his religious belief, he stayed his course, never wavered and stuck to it. He came back to regain his world heavyweight championship title, so religion has nothing to do with it, just your stick-to-it-ive-ness.

So, it is not empowering to claim one's upbringing, harsh conditions, abuse or even torture if, in the light of a goal or dream, one is persistent, as in the case of John McCain, who was a prison of war. He was captured and tortured, and after his release, persevered and persisted in his undertakings to gain a seat as a senator and achieved repeatedly.

There are obstacles to be transcended on one's way to attainment as stated above. So let the rest of the examples be a guide for you as to the people who have persevered and persisted on their journey to success.

The now famous and successful Sylvester Stallone was down and out, suicidal before his first cheap $200 salary porn movie role. Michael Jordan was cut from his high school basketball team and was told by his coach he could not play basketball. These are just a few of the people who experienced doors closed in their faces and others thereby holding them back.

Fred Astaire, was refused a role in show business. It was stated in the evaluation of Astaire's first screen test: "Can't act. Can't sing. Balding. Can dance a little." (www.IMDb.com)

Oprah experienced hardships during her upbringing and she transcended these and persevered persistently.

Napoleon Hill spent twenty years of perseverance, researching the deep teaching and understanding and publishing the knowledge he gathered in his book, *THINK and GROW RICH*, which has revolutionized and changed many lives. He did not let his being an ex-convict stop him.

Anthony Robbins has undergone failures in his life, even as a motivational speaker. But through his perseverance and persistence, he emerged stronger, wiser and better and made an even bigger impact on lives all over the world.

Mahatma Gandhi persevered after telling the British it was time to leave India and achieved his goal. He did not have the wealth, money or a background of luxury to achieve his goal. In fact, he just had the loin cloth which wrapped his nakedness. He refused to give up on his dream. You are no different.

Martin Luther King persisted despite the danger he faced during his challenges of the status quo; and he changed America for the better, paving the way for people like Barack Obama to become the first African American in the White House.

Betsy Ross stuck to her guns and refused to move until she accomplished what she was after, when it was dangerous to do so, likewise Nelson Mandela. It is uncanny that there seems to be a great force which comes along to aide you, once you set yourself unwavering to a task. The force comes and sees you through. Just stay the course – persevere and be persistent!

It states in the good book that, 'no one is worthy of the kingdom who sets his hand on a plough and looks back' – which can be interpreted as staying the course with perseverance and persistence in achieving your goal.

Wayne Dyer, after completing his first book, *Your Erroneous Zones*, was refused publishing by many publishers, so he self-published it. He was persistent to be successful, and he bought his own books to spark activities around his writing until the populace and publishers recognized his talent and were willing to publish him subsequently.

Jack Canfield, now a well-known and famous bestselling author was refused some 140 times by publishers when trying to have his first book, *Chicken Soup for the Soul*, published. He never gave up and persisted for some 18 months. You see, you can savor the flavor of a door being slammed in someone's face.

There are people out there who do that for whatever reasons – prejudice, discrimination, jealousy, ignorance, to name a few. All these people did not let the failure to get what they wanted stop them. They persisted. They persevered. They stayed the course. They focused on their goal and they transcended and achieved.

Lots of millionaires were school drop outs. Some dropped out because they were bored and some realized very early what they wanted and went for it. Either way, lack of education was not a deterrent. They just persevered and persisted in their undertakings to achieve success.

Nelson Mandela, in wanting freedom for his people, stayed the course with persistence, perseverance and endurance for 27 years of imprisonment to pay the price of his dream – realizing that the goal is mostly achieved as soon as it is started. It is like the first step in a thousand-mile journey which makes it less than a thousand miles. Abraham Lincoln was defeated many times during his run for office as a political leader. He repeatedly ran for the same office until he succeeded. His determination helped him overcome the stumbling blocks, until he achieved the highest office in the United States. Now, that is perseverance and persistence for you.

Neither bankruptcy nor criminal record is a game stopper for perseverance and persistence. It is not a well-known fact that one of the world-famous speakers and authors, who brought the world a deep life-changing education and proof, whose authorship is one of the most read books – second to the bible – was incarcerated with a criminal record and declared bankruptcy. Napoleon Hill persevered through 20 years of research and published the renowned book, *THINK and GROW RICH*, which has been very successful—even up to now.

What does it take to be successful? It takes a combination of things, all achievable. There are steps. The first step is knowing what one wants and desires. It may be fighting for a cause, righting a wrong, invention or creativity – as in discovery of what may help our growth and make life comfortable for humanity. It may be a dream, a passion or an innate ability. The second step is decision. And there are other steps not in consideration at this time, but the best of them all is persistence. It is the best all-rounder, the most important contributor.

After making your decision, then you want to persistently take action. It just so happens that there is nothing which the mind can conceive (conjure up, dream up) that the dreamer cannot achieve. The necessary ingredients to achieving the set perception (goal) is already there before the person can even come up with the goal. How often have you had something come up for consideration, and you asked yourself, "I wonder how come there are no such-and-such?" No sooner, you start to see the same thing on television being advertised, and you almost beat yourself up that you did not pursue your dream/idea to fruition when it welled up in front of you.

I no longer lament such faith any longer. I am simultaneously working on many projects because I now know how things work. I get up from sleep and write ideas down now with excited determination to complete each one of the projects. Who needs boredom when just thinking of our dreams is exciting? You are the beneficiary of this same knowledge if this is your first privilege with it. Many of us are not fortunate to learn this at any early age. Now, the door is open and many people are discovering that the powerful human spirit, which can achieve whatever it can perceive and persevere in with persistence, can win the goal.

Use persistence to keep on keeping on. When the going gets tough, the tough gets going. Remember the picture of the frog and the crane. The crane has the frog's head in its mouth, about to swallow the frog, and the frog squeezes the neck of the crane below where his head is, and escapes. Never give up!

Stick-to-it-ive-ness: I am not saying that you should foolishly or stubbornly stick to one way of doing the same thing and getting nowhere. I am talking of persistence in achieving good outcomes, being successful, adjusting, rediscovering and reinventing, with patience, calmness, fortitude, vision, and hope; just stay the course. It is being mindful in prayer (which is constant meditation – just marinating in one's desire), and focused.

NEITHER LISTEN NOR CONSIDER THE OBSTACLES OF NAYSAYERS

The saboteurs, who neither want nor can fathom your success, have no desire to achieve and will do anything to keep anybody else from reaching their goals. They will sabotage their own family members, even their own children. Some husbands sabotage their wives and vice versa. Just stay the course and be persistent in achieving your dreams. Thomas Edison and Nicholas Tesla spent thousands of hours in their laboratories to achieve their vision and humanity enjoys and thanks them for their perseverance and persistence.

Keep these reminders on hand on your way to achieving your goals, successes, and freedom:
1) Set goals from your desires and not somebody else's. It is better if your goal is your passion.
2) Enjoy your passion along the way, making your work into play.
3) Be careful and mindful of, and stay away from, naysayers.
4) Remember that 'A journey of a thousand miles starts with the first step.' (Lao Tzu)
5) Do something daily towards the fulfilment of your goals.
6) Neither listen to nor even allow anyone to tell you what you can achieve for yourself.

7) No dream is too big or too small – it is your dream, make it happen.

8) It is never too late to start to persist in your dream to achievement.

9) You are never too old. Go for it now.

10) Persistence – do not give up on your dream. Never give up on yourself.

©Copyright 2017.　Dr. Jonathan Agbebiyi, MD, MBA.

About Dr. Jonathan

Dr. Jonathan Agbebiyi has always been an advocate and helper of people, particularly the underdog and the underserved. His childhood experience and training in organizations like Scouting, Boys Brigade, Choir and as a gold medalist in Man-O-War-Bay training program contributed to his orientation to discipline, service and persistence.

He obtained his MD degree from the University of Michigan, Ann Arbor and later graduated from the University of Phoenix with an MBA degree. At the beginning of his medical career as an Obstetrician and Gynecologist, he was one of the few physicians who supported, served and cared for the indigent patient population during the inception of Arizona's AHCCCS indigent care program, helping to bring the program to success. He practiced medicine as an obstetrician and gynecologist for many years and has incorporated supportive practices like Nutritional Weight Control (a medical weight-loss program), which he created. In addition, he authored an adjunctive motivational audio program he called, *The Gift of Lite* – a motivational program for choice and success – to help his patients lose the stubborn remaining excess weight after the delivery of their babies.

Dr. Agbebiyi was the founder and CEO of Harmony Health Choice, and he, as needs be, incorporated additional practices into his medical practice to help pregnant patients who had challenges with addiction. This supportive addiction medicine practice was later extended to benefit other types of patient populations needing such support. In addition, he was the CEO and program director of "My Visiting Physicians", which provided care for homebound, infirm patients.

Jonathan's segued career is a continuation of his support of people. He now centers his services on giving back from his accumulated knowledge and understanding of many years of various life experiences and challenges, studies, training and diverse religious and philosophical practices. His goal is to help his clients build a better and easier life by imparting these nuggets and understanding of key information and knowledge previously mostly obscured, and now necessary to be delivered in a way easily comprehensible and digested so that it can be utilized by people for changing their lives for the better. Dr. Agbebiyi is also a trained and experienced hypnotherapist, and uses this skill to support the medical treatments that help patients transcend their issues when undergoing treatment like surgery, and to help them recover easier and faster after such treatment.

Dr. Agbebiyi is an Omega training graduate. He is well-versed in philosophy, comparative religious studies and coaching. He is trained in NLP and is a first

Dan (Black Belt) in the Martial Arts discipline of Taekwondo. He contributes and supports many charitable organizations. He is the founder and chairman of Harmony Endowment Foundation, a non-profit charitable organization focused on helping the underserved and underprivileged in many areas of the world, especially in developing countries, that espouses finding and supplying clean drinkable water, food, clothing and education.

Dr. Agbebiyi is a fine artist, supported a commissioned artist, producing bronze statues of Young Native America Girls, including – "The Three Graces" (Love, Hope and Faith) – which is located at the entrance to the Paradise Valley Mall in Arizona, and he enjoys and is an avid supporter of the Arts.

You can connect with Dr. Agbebiyi at:
- exproserve1@exproserve.com
- www.facebook.com/Exproserve-1716062361756974/
- www.twitter.com/Exproserve

CHAPTER 20

FROM MILITARY LIFE TO THE CIVILIAN WORLD

BY LEFFORD FATE

If you work hard on your job, you can make a living.
If you work on yourself, you can make a life?

In my military career, I've known many bright, hardworking and dedicated Airmen who didn't transition well and ended up in jobs that sucked the life out of them. They took positions far below their skill level and ended up depressed, sick and lost. Some made good money but weren't happy. Some enjoyed their off-duty time but couldn't make ends meet. Some were leaving the military after 2 years others after 20, all were fearful of the process. This is understandable. To live the military life – whether soldier, sailor, airman, coastguardsman or marine - it is a life of high-stress that demands a lot from you; it requires a heightened sense of awareness, being constantly watchful and on guard and, in many cases, seeing a fair share of death and destruction.

The average military member has spent most of their time at war. Whether in combat or in support, few years or many, they become accustomed to this high stress life – always on edge and alert – accustomed to horrors that most civilians can't imagine. It becomes all they know. For those who are not on the battlefield, the job can still be demanding, high operations tempo, filling in for those deployed, being understaffed, can be exhausting both mentally and psychologically.

These same people come to the end of their service, though excited, suddenly are anxious about their transition. Civilian life is nothing like military life. I have known many, that come out confused as to how to conduct themselves in the "real world", how to 'fit back into society' and how to make a life for themselves. The unknown scared them greatly. Many were very excited about leaving the military and were so full of hope but did not make any plans for a transition and, unfortunately, struggled with civilian life. A few months after leaving service they still had not found what they wanted and were living with regret, despair and disappointment.

How can you make your transition easier? There is much that can be done to ease the process and make it much less painful. But, you must have a plan.

Let's talk about a very serious issue that affects many in our society but especially many transitioning from the military, Post-Traumatic Stress Disorder or PTSD. According to: www.ptsdunited.org, "PTSD is a psychobiological mental disorder that can affect survivors not only of combat experience, but terror attacks, natural disasters, serious accidents, assault or abuse, or even sudden and major emotional losses." PTSD doesn't affect every service member; however, it certainly affects a fair share. According to www.veteransandptsd.com, "nearly 50% of American soldiers that return from war have PTSD but are not diagnosed. Of those that are diagnosed, the numbers doubled after one year of being back in civilian life." For example, "According to RAND, at least 20% of Iraq and Afghanistan veterans have PTSD and/or depression." It also says that "19% of veterans may have traumatic brain injury and that "out of half that seek treatment, only half of them get the treatment they need."

In addition, we learn that "PTSD is the third most prevalent psychiatric diagnosis among veterans using VA Hospitals." Along with PTSD there is a relationship between military members coming back into civilian life and suicide? From www.veteransandptsd.com we learn that 5,000 to 8,000 former military members kill themselves each year. That works out to about 22 vets a day that are committing suicide, Why? This statistic brings us to realize that military members who do not transition properly can sometimes truly burn out.

Many falsely assume that PTSD only affects marines or soldiers. In the army, referencing data from years back (which have most certainly increased over the years), there are approximately 67% PTSD cases in the Army, in the Air Force there is 9%, in the Navy there is 11% PTSD cases and the Marines have roughly 13%. "In the last year alone, the cases of PTSD in the military have jumped 50%." According to www.ptsd.va.gov, "11-20% of veterans from the Operations Iraqi Freedom (OFI) and Enduring Freedom (OEF) have PTSD." These statistics are scary. More to the point, making the transition from the military to civilian life, it is important to have an idea of the statistics. Don't let yourself be a statistic. It is important to realize that if you have PTSD, you are not alone. Even if you don't have PTSD and are just anxious about a transition into civilian life, you are not alone. There are people whose sole mission is to help you. How can you transition? Where do you start and what should you do first?

Considering for a moment that you or someone you know is a veteran with PTSD, here are some steps that can be taken to fight against it. First, be aware of the symptoms of PTSD. Some symptoms are strong and unwanted memories of the event, bad dreams, emotional numbness, intense guilt or worry, angry outbursts, feeling "on edge" and avoiding thoughts and situations that are a reminder of the trauma. If any of these symptoms sound familiar, seek help. Do not try to ignore them or keep your concerns to yourself. Talk to someone you trust and care for... this could be a family member or friend. Visit a VA Hospital, speak to a counselor or mental health professional. These steps can be a great beginning for your healing.

Let's take a break from talking about PTSD and discuss those that feel anxious and lost transitioning back into civilian life due solely to the transition itself. No matter what your level or stance was within the military, the following are universal steps – from the individual who served two years and saw little to the thirty-year veteran that saw a lot. These are helpful steps that served me well and I am confident will serve you in the same positive way.

1. **First, develop your transition plan. Where do you start and what should you do first?**

It's possible you might need a home and a car. You may already have both, but if you don't, contact the Veteran's Administration or speak to family and friends about your search to put down roots. Look into different options you earned as a Veteran, there are many. Assuming you secured a home and a car before you got out, let's focus on your new career for a moment. Much of what is involved in finding a job follows a rational decision-making model.

2. The Process

In the military, you are accustomed to setting goals, developing plans, and focusing on the mission. Therefore, the career-finding process should make sense to you. The career search steps involve investigation, preparing and writing a resume, and learning how to contact the right employers. To be successful in finding your career, learn to implement each of these steps that involve planning, organizational, and communications skills.

3. The Best Jobs for the 21st Century

The job market is constantly changing. Today, individuals with the right education, skills, and experience are in a better position to find good jobs that should lead to career advancement in the years ahead. You can find a list of the fastest-growing occupations till 2024 on the U.S. Department of Labor's website at www.bls.gov. You may be saying "I don't have the education or skills that others have." – that's fine. Your time in the military has equipped you with a great set of skills – You rise early, stay in shape, and listen, and follow instructions. These are great assets for any employer.

You are also respected as a veteran and are intelligent. Being part of the military is no easy feat, give yourself credit for that. The training and intelligence that is needed to work in the military transfers well in civilian life. Maybe your resume isn't very long. Showcase the skills you learned within the military. If need be, invest in a company that specializes in Resume writing. Do not undersell yourself – being part of the military means that you have skills that many civilians don't have. Employers are interested in your skill set and they know that you could be a positive influence on their staff. By nature, you are a hard-worker with incredible mental strength. What's more, the better part of the population has a lot of respect for your service to our country. These key points are to your advantage.

4. Develop an Action-Oriented Timeline

As with any military operation, it's important to establish a timeline and be disciplined in the execution of your planned activities. Developing a sound yet flexible search plan is critical to conducting a successful career search. The time spent planning and organizing your activities will result in a far more effective job search.

5. Your Job Search Competency

Before you acquire names, addresses, and phone numbers of potential employers, you should possess the necessary job search knowledge and skills for gathering and using job information effectively. Valuable awareness is gained by examining your present level of job search competency. As stated earlier, the military has given you a large skill set that more than qualifies you for many jobs. Think about the skills you have and jot them down. Take note of skills you may still want to learn and you feel would be necessary if going after a specific career build.

The military offers great training. This was a step that helped me quite a bit. I took a look at everything I was offered and started to ask myself, how could this not only help me while on active duty, but what could it offer to the civilian sector? I have discovered that most things directly or indirectly carry over once you leave the service. Take a few minutes now and think about something you did today. Ask yourself what you learned from the experience and how could you use it to craft a better tomorrow? You might be surprised at what you will come up with.

One of the main things I learned was if I wanted to be successful I needed to study successful people. I read everything I could from Anthony Robbins to Zig Ziglar. I tried to take something out of each of the books I read to help me get ready for my life after the military. There are an unlimited amount of resources and professionals in society that can help you. I discovered that many of the most successful people started from humble backgrounds. Somehow, before my journey of discovery, I thought that only the ones born into wealthy families could be great. This is simply not true. I learned that most of them had to overcome some type of adversity.

Not only did I read, I started asking people that I knew and trusted who had already retired or were planning on getting out what they did and why. I started having conversations about the process. Talking about leaving the military took some of the fear and concern out of the process. Understand that hundreds of thousands of people have gone before you and many have done well, so if they can, so can you.

Ask yourself the following questions and tackle each question individually. These questions can assist you in your transition. Remember, take a breath. You are part of the military, even as a vet and that takes a special person. Your Success Starts Today. Go and get it!

- ➤ What is your dream?
- ➤ What are your strengths?
- ➤ What do you love doing?
- ➤ What are your mental, emotional and financial needs?
- ➤ What is available in the area you are going to live?
- ➤ How much money do you need?
- ➤ Do you have a good network of professionals that can guide you?
- ➤ What/Who do you need to become to get what you want out of life?
- ➤ How confident are you with becoming the person you want to be?
- ➤ Are you willing to go back to school?

∞

About Lefford

Professionally, Mr. Lefford Fate has led, mentored, and served thousands of military members and their families. He spent nearly 31 years in the US Air Force and retired as Command Chief of the 20th Fighter Wing. A Chief is the top of the enlisted structure. It is the highest enlisted rank you can achieve, a great honor. As Command Chief, Lefford was the senior ranking enlisted person on the base and was responsible for the care, development and welfare of 5000+ people.

Since retiring from the military, he has worked in various capacities. He was the program director for a geriatric outpatient mental health program, Director for Health Service within the SC Department of Corrections and is currently the Director of Support Services for the City of Sumter, South Carolina. Lefford is certified to facilitate, speak, train and coach individuals and groups in the areas of leadership development, professional skills and personal growth

Mr. Fate is a husband, father, and grandfather. He knows it is not always easy to juggle our list of daily responsibilities. This makes it all the more important to have a structured, practical plan in place to avoid becoming overwhelmed. He holds a Master's Degree in Human Relations and a Bachelor's Degree in Social Psychology. Each day, he models the core values of *Integrity* first, *Service* before self and *Excellence* in all that he does. Lefford has learned tools and skills to enhance his own productivity, development and decision-making skills in order to create a more balanced lifestyle for both himself and his family. He greatly looks forward to sharing with you the leadership skills that he has learned over the last three decades.

According to John Maxwell, 'the two greatest days in a person's life are the day he or she was born and the day he or she discovers why they were born.' Lefford believes there is a "why" for everyone; that each of us was created with the potential to achieve greatness, to make a difference in the world, to add value to others, and as a result, experience a full and rewarding life. For over 30 years, Mr. Fate's purpose was to defend our nation, and now that purpose is helping people discover their life's purpose and grow to their full potential. You have met your Fate; let's walk into your destiny. If you want help in becoming the best version of YOU, Lefford Fate can be reached at: www.sumtercoaching.com or leffordfate.com.

Here are some websites that may help you along your path of transitioning from the military into civilian life. (You can also download the Military Transition app on your iPhone or Android phone.)

- www.careerproplus.com/Transition-Resume

- www.clearancejobs.com
- www.makingtheconnection.net
- www.operationwearehere.com
- www.military.com

CHAPTER 21

SUCCESS: WEAR SEER SUCKER IN THE WINTER

BY MELANIE E. BRATCHER, Ph.D.

I sat there crying, hurt from all that had happened, from all that I'd wanted to do. I missed my classrooms and my students and the critical and comical and painful engagement of topics that mattered and still matter to me. I needed a break from it but I missed it. I'm sure this sounds really successful, right?

I knew I'd touched lives and I also questioned whether or not I had touched lives. That's really the only thing that I wanted to do; touch lives with beauty, but it was all snatched away, so I sat there crying. All I had worked so long and hard and lovingly on was gone, and it seemed like it was not coming back to me or that it was out of reach or being withheld. Half of my life, wiped away with a smug, four-paragraph letter, handed to me by people who couldn't look me in my eyes.

You've probably heard, "Be careful what you ask for, you may just get it." What's interesting is that I had not been listening to myself, to what I'd been asking for, for quite some time. I usually asked for it in the form of statements like, "I want to teach yoga," and "I'm a speaker, a performer," and "I want to see the world and teach." I'd been told, in many different ways, that what I wanted to teach was not appealing to the masses. But, I knew better. I had higher expectations of the world and thus a bigger responsibility and that is daunting. Again, sounds really successful, right?

Left, ... I was left, and I turned left, and left again, and again, until I found my way out of a maze. Then I realized I was in another maze, the one that led me here, well there, sitting and crying.

A year ago, I sold and gave away all the stuff, packed my car and drove to California. In that year I completed three programs, two in Yoga and one in Law of Attraction Life Coaching. I'd also traveled to Alabama, Indonesia, La Jolla, New Mexico, St. Maarten and Mexico City, and still had Carson City, Atlanta, and Philadelphia awaiting my arrival. Now, what I experienced, and what I had yet to experience in each of those places, spans the spectrum of Shadow and Light Work, Emotional and Physical Fitness Testing, and a considerable amount of BS trickery. And even though I sat there crying, I had to ask myself, "How in the world did you get here, there, and back to here and what are you going to do with all these experiences?" The only thing I knew for sure is it had been an exchange of stuff for experiences and new knowledge. Why was I crying? Because.

Are you still waiting on the successful part? Me too, in a way. However, I came across a beautiful nugget in Christy Whitman's Law of Attraction Life Coach program: "The secret to all success is keeping yourself happy." I, like you, have also encountered the idea that success is the trappings of an image of financial wealth—married with two children, luxury cars, and a well-ordered life; including a beautiful house/home. Those images are extremely appealing. However, what I was discovering is that success is a state of mind. Of course, that is not a new idea or invention. But oh! It is an experience.

While my travels included some leisure and much needed rest, they were ultimately life courses in my journey of introspection. I had to look deep within and discover/uncover some darkness and some more light. My first Falling Awake workshop by Dave Ellis (who also wrote the book) is where I encountered a powerful way of orchestrating self-realization with network building. The practices we did at the workshop opened me up to talk with strangers about hard life experiences and to dream bigger in order to share the beauty of my hard life experiences.

Henare and Kate O'Brien's Game Changer retreat was for me a Shamanistic adventure into Shadow work and self-realization. I had been on a long journey of grief and what I uncovered in their retreat was harsh. Years previous, my closest student was killed and I realized that my own thoughts of suicide were entangled with feeling like I had cheated in life. I couldn't understand why a young beautiful woman who was a rising star was taken while I, who was at an extremely pained point in life, was still alive. I was angry at the loss and at myself for being a coward. I had an opportunity (in the trial that ensued) to stand up for compassion and a new way of justice, and I couldn't, that is, I didn't. So, I carried even more grief and felt even lower. However, the mere uttering of that realization during the retreat released a tremendous amount of pain for me.

At Lisa Nichols' "Speak and Write to Make Millions" conference, a high energy journey into the art of motivational speaking and business building, I was immersed in a sea of big dreams that uplifted my spirits and reintroduced me to an efficacy in human relating. I began to more clearly see how I could merge my academic background with my current life lessons and pointedly talk with people about what I wanted and have to offer.

These highlights occurred while I was taking three certification programs. Each demanded varied levels of physical, emotional, mental and spiritual endurance. I was stretched, am still being stretched, in ways that seem impossible. There's still a lifetime of studying to do and to borrow from Yogic terminology, a vinyasa (special order or placement of breath and movement) with which to do it. I was learning how to wait to inhale; no small feat and I have a long way to go toward mastery. Considering that two years prior, I was still sometimes thinking about not breathing anymore at all, to me it was all a great feat. Everything happened because of a need to express. I wanted and needed to say everything, and couldn't, didn't. Are you a success if you succeed in not killing yourself? Although that's a joke for some people; yes, you are a success. The shift in my state of mind and the intensifying quality of thoughts, though gradual, was success. Something in me urged a deeper look inside and outside of me. I was seeing everything I wanted and needed to say and share.

Here are eleven realizations about success I need to share with you:

1. See it all—everything that you see. Observe, become a scientist by virtue of the definition of science – to observe. See yourself

in everything and everyone. Admire what is beautiful to you. Be horrified by what is not beautiful to you and move to transform that in yourself.

2. Embrace every emotion and feeling you experience and give some time to it; study it. Mine each feeling for gold, believing that you can offer something beautiful and salient to the world from what you discover/uncover. If you have ever had a really long hug, recall what it did for you. Recall how it allowed you, prompted you to finally just melt and release and merge with the other person; with yourself. Recall how you moved in the world after that long hug; embrace. If you haven't had a really long hug, go get one right now. Stop reading and go hug someone for a really long time.

3. Engage your pain and your joy. Get engaged to it. Put a ring on it. Marry it and commit to a forever of knowing, loving, and harnessing your own intensity. Grow your intensity and use it to blaze trails that defy (but acknowledge) pain and amplify (really acknowledge) joy.

4. Recognize the fact that your wildest dreams are possible and probable and then rearrange your life to move toward your dream. Life has a funny way of rearranging things for you as well. Feel it all out and add your own rearrangement. Go for it. The only thing you regret is what you did not do that you wanted to do. In the midst of the rearrangement(s), mess up (a lot) and keep going. Figure it out slowly, fast, out of order, or with great confusion; but go for it.

5. Surrender to the circumstances that both scare the crap out of you and simultaneously pull your heart strings while stimulating your most creative headiness. Surrender, sometimes very slowly, and then realize that we are always surrendering. Be sure you are doing so according to your own vision.

6. Satisfy yourself! Yes, curiosity killed the cat, but satisfaction brought her back. Get curious about any and everything you've imagined and desired doing. Dive into your curiosities, especially when life presents an opportunity or rips apart your known life or because you know deep inside that you have to explore more and expand yourself. This comes at a price and a cost to you but who better to invest in than yourself, that you may subsequently invest in others.

7. Urge your deepest truths to come clear to you and then stand in those truths. No matter what comes at you, know that it is a test of your conviction and courage to stand by your truths. Express your truths with love regardless of current trends and believe that your stance will magnetize people to you, your message, your product, your voice. We all need to witness people who follow the urging of their souls.

8. Cuss. Cuss a little. Cuss a lot. Think of following your dream as a title in a "(Fill-In-The-Blank) For Dummies" book series. At times, the blank is filled with words that describe 'Aha' moments and then there are times when the blank is filled with choicest explicative, mostly a response to pain. And honestly, only follow this advice if you were raised with a benevolent sense of humor.

9. Keep going. Keep going. Keep going! And rest, but keep going!

10. Endure your own fear until the fear dissipates. It is easy to think of dismissing fear, but it has some valuable information for you. You can work to dissipate the fear with a variety of techniques and processes, but your endurance in general is greatened by understanding what your fear is telling you. So, endure fear in order to heal it; transform it to recognize the light and power of your love.

11. Retouch your inner image. See yourself as varied images of success and merge those images into a balance and harmony that is unique to your vision of an ideal life; a life of purpose and play and powerful peace that can touch and serve others.

I have learned that resting and reading (to learn) are equally important in prioritizing your time. When things are crazy or seem crazy, remember, "It's happening for me!" Doubts are your friends; indicators that you have more to be and do. If you get stuck in doubt know that you are living in fear, so acknowledge the fear, look deeper inside for your vision and the powerful feelings that come with your vision.

Find techniques and practices that move you away from being stuck. Life coaching is a great and viable option. Movement in various aspects of your life can alleviate feeling stuck and help you identify how to transfer good feelings and experiences into the space that doubt occupies. For me in particular, Yoga Works. It gave me a way to create more space, everywhere.

Success is a state of mind, a state of being. It is an ever-proceeding process. It is seeing and seeking and taking everything in so that you can share all of it, knowing that someone will benefit from your rest and reading and practice and energy.

And then. . . *simply wear seer sucker in the winter.*

About Dr. Melanie

Melanie E. Bratcher, Ph.D. wears many outfits as a published author, writer, professor, arts advocate, public speaker, singer, yoga teacher, dancer, and cultural consultant. She has been teaching children of all ages and at the collegiate level for over twenty years. Her passions are singing (especially in the car), learning, and guiding people into deep thought and feeling about important and controversial issues. Her latest pursuits include becoming a RYT-500 — Registered Yoga Teacher, certified Thai Yoga Bodywork Practitioner, and certified Law of Attraction Life Coach. She enjoys teaching yoga and sharing its wellness benefits.

A caring teacher, Melanie puts safety first and focuses on healthy alignment to assist students in having a well-rounded critical thinking experience, yoga practice, energy work session, and/or life coaching adventure. She brings more than twenty years of movement instruction to each class, workshop, seminar, and retreat she conducts and she believes in the power of experiential learning. Melanie shares a variety of wellness modalities with students.

Dr. Bratcher is no stranger to tough breaks and both hard and smart work. She is advancing to bring balance and harmony to women's issues and racial and cultural divisions, and blends ancient traditions with contemporary research to facilitate real, loving, and in-depth experiences for her students and clients. If you are a Jazz and Blues lover and are intrigued about African culture and race-gender issues check out her first scholarly book, *The Words and Songs of Bessie Smith, Billie Holiday, and Nina Simone.* If you are curious and into music, culture, and a blend of ancient and New Age approaches to life and lifestyle keep an eye out for her upcoming books, *Church of the Holy Cuss Word* and *Oops, I Dropped It: A Tale of Trials and Trails.*

To find out more about what this sassy, sometimes silly, sensual and serious woman is up to and can offer you or your organization, visit: MelangeVibe.com for listings about workshops, speaking engagements, seminars, yoga classes and to schedule private/small group yoga sessions, Thai Yoga Bodywork sessions, and Life Coaching sessions.

Her mantra is: *Remember, I celebrate you.*

CHAPTER 22

GET GUTSY AND GET GOING TO GET WHAT YOU WANT

BY PAT OBUCHOWSKI

*The way in which we think of ourselves has everything to do
with how our world sees us and how we see ourselves
successfully acknowledged by the world.*
~ Arlene Rankin

Have you ever had someone say something to you that shook your world and made you feel worth less than what you believed you were worth? Well, I have and here's what I did about it.

Early in my career, I was working in business at an international company. It was January, the dreaded "Personnel Management Performance Review" time. I walked into my boss' office, and sat at the round table where we usually worked. He got up from behind his desk, walked over to the table and sat directly across from me. He seemed hesitant as he handed me the written review. As I read the review, my jaw dropped, my eyes kept getting bigger, and I sat up a bit straighter.

I had excelled in every possible category. I was ecstatic. I knew I worked really hard that year and was so pleased to see that someone recognized me for my work, especially someone whose opinion I highly respected. I was really seen. I was recognized as a great contributor. I was valued.

I was excited and ready to continue doing my excellent work.

But then there was a very uncomfortable silence. He looked at me and just said, "Unfortunately, the range of raises this year are lower than last year."

I knew this was not going to be good. "You'll be getting a 2% raise."

I was stunned. This raise was nowhere close to what I thought equaled the amount of effort I had put into my work. It did not come close to compensating me for the process changes I made that saved the company money; for the many recommendations I made that were put into place; or for the many extra hours I worked.

I looked at him and felt my throat tighten, my body stiffen, and the tears welling up. We just stared at each other for what seemed like an eternity. I took a very deep breath, felt my body pulling together and a tiny little voice came out of me and said, "I can't talk about this right now." I got up and walked out of the room.

I immediately went to the bathroom, sat on the toilet, and let the tears roll. I couldn't get my head around it. I was raised to believe that all you needed to do to get recognized was to keep your head down, work hard, and wait for the inevitable recognition that would be tossed at my feet.

But, I had just seen first-hand that this wasn't necessarily true. I sat there and thought, "I am worth more than this." I sat there a little longer and thought, "I am worth more than this." Then, drying my tears, I stood up and said out loud, in that bathroom, "I am worth more than this!"

I left the stall, walked over to the sink and looked at myself for a while in the mirror. I was surprised to see a strong, confident and well, gutsy woman gazing right back at me. Here was a woman willing to claim her place and her immense value in the world. And that woman was me. I went back to my office, sat down and I started to write. I am worth more, I am worth more, I am worth more. This led to me writing why I thought so.

I left the pad of paper in my desk drawer, went home, and came back the next day clearly prepared with what I was going to say to my boss. I was fully prepared psychologically to leave my job if I didn't get what I thought I was worth. This was that important to me.

First thing that morning, I went into his office and boldly said, "We need to talk."

We did talk and at the end of the conversation he looked at me and said, "Pat, that was gutsy of you."

"You got that right," I proclaimed. So... what did I learn throughout all this? Sitting there in that bathroom was a turning point for me. It was right then that I consciously realized I had a choice: to cave or to claim the power to claim my life. I realized that no one, absolutely no one, had the power to make me feel worthless (unless I gave that power to him or her). It was at that moment I realized that "getting gutsy" was the only way to make my world rather than allowing it to make me.

It was the moment I knew, really knew, I had a choice in everything I did and in determining, for me, what was acceptable and what was not.

By the way, I got exactly the raise I wanted.

> *The most common way people give up their power is by*
> *thinking they don't have any.*
> ~ Alice Walker

Fast forward to today. Being a woman in male-dominated industries always had its unique challenges for me. When I coach young women in business, I see there are still a lot of the same issues today that I experienced many years ago.

As I think about the reasons why not that much has changed, some of the things I notice are the following:

1. There is a lack of female role models and mentors in top management. Catalyst research[1] shows that the labor force participation of women has increased over 28% since 1978, but women only make up 16.3% of CEO positions and 34.1% of Senior Management roles in 2015-2016. Those that we are able to observe and be impacted by are still predominately male.

---

1. http://www.catalyst.org/knowledge/statistical-overview-women-workforce

2. Lack of sponsors. Mentors are important to success, but a sponsor is a champion for you in the workplace. This means they can provide visibility, as well as remove barriers and vouch for your work when it comes to promotions and other opportunities. Again, this is still male dominated. With sponsors, it's not who you know, it's who knows you.

3. Exclusion of informal network opportunities. Women are often excluded from what is still the 'good ol' boys' network. Informal networking is key to having social and business connections that advance your career. These opportunities are usually oriented to males, as we like to be in a social environment with those who are similar to us.

4. Stigma about senior male/younger female. Yes, sexism does still exist. Just take a look at what is going on in places such as Google and Uber.[2] Because of this, the senior management males sometimes avoid the younger females, and hence, the circle with men supporting men continues.

Other reasons are:

5. Outdated beliefs of women's leadership skills being 'too soft'.

6. Women still have primary house/child responsibility.

7. Women perceive limitations and barriers in their professional environment and ask, "Is this important?"

And the list goes on. . .

In May 2014, Katty Kay and Claire Shipman wrote an article for *The Atlantic*[3] titled, The Confidence Gap. Their research showed evidence that women are less self-assured than men, and that to succeed, confidence matters as much as competence.

"A growing body of evidence shows just how devastating this lack of

---

2. https://www.theguardian.com/money/2017/sep/02/lawyers-silicon-valley-sexism-worse-google-uber-lawless-sisters.

3. https://www.theatlantic.com/magazine/archive/2014/05/the-confidence-gap/359815/

confidence can be. Success, it turns out, correlates just as closely with confidence as it does with competence. No wonder that women, despite all our progress, are still woefully underrepresented at the highest levels. All of that is the bad news. The good news is that with work, confidence can be acquired. Which means that the confidence gap, in turn, can be closed."

But having the experience of the challenge and reward I had in my story to be gutsy along with knowing and believing in my own self-worth along the journey, finding this confidence to speak up for me has helped me become the woman and successful businesswoman I am today.

The question isn't who's going to let me; it's who is going to stop me.
~ Ayn Rand

At times, I can feel myself step back into thinking I am a little less worthy, less smarter, and a little less experienced than someone else. And yes, this still happens. Or when those gremlin, saboteur, and monkey-mind voices start screaming in my head and filling me up with self-doubt that makes me want to back down, I take a deep breath, stand up and take a power pose position[4] and use these *Top Ten Tips* to remind myself of the power and talent and skill and strengths I have.

Tip #10. In my Catholic school teachings, a tactic was used to keep us behaving and staying in our place. We were told if we were bad, they were putting it in our "permanent record." In college, we were told it would go into the files potential employers would review. In companies, it was always the dreaded personnel file where all our badness would be collected. Well, don't worry, they may go in there, but no one, absolutely no one, looks at them. So, don't let that stop you.

Tip #9. Master Your Strengths. If you do, no one will care about your weaknesses. My career has been what I call a portfolio career. About every 18 months I would be looking for something new and challenging to do. I always questioned this pattern as my friends would get hired and stick to one path. Quite a few years ago, I took

---

4. https://www.ted.com/talks/amy_cuddy_your_body_language_shapes_who_you_are

an online assessment called Strengths Finders 2.0[5] and found that learning is one of my top five strengths. That was my light bulb moment. The answer for my career movement every 18 months is that I learned all I could in one area and was on to the next. This now, is one of my greatest strengths that I use as part of my brand.

Tip #8. Remember crappy experiences make for scrappy stories later on. Look at challenges and what feels like big losses from the perspective of 'in the future', you will see it as a "You're-not-going-to-believe-this-story..." factor. Just like my story above.

Tip #7. Appreciate those around you and show them your appreciation. A key thing is that you are modeling behaviors and what is acceptable and not acceptable all the time. Make sure you are a great model.

Tip #6. Live by your values no matter what. Know them and never compromise them. Use them as your guide and stand up for what matters most to you. If you compromise your values, your respect for yourself will decrease. Be sure you are living them every single day.

Tip #5. Hold everything lightly and not too seriously. Remember you are not saving babies. Unless, of course, you are.

Tip #4. Admit what you don't know. . . don't lie or make it up. People will know.

Tip #3. Find true, honest and loyal friends who will tell you what you're great at and keep telling you what you're great at when you forget.

Tip #2. Always prepare for Crucial Conversations.[6]
Ask yourself and be very clear on your answers:

- What do I want for me?
- What do I want for the other person?
- What do I want for the relationship?

---

5. https://www.gallupstrengthscenter.com/home/en-us/strengthsfinder?utm_
   source=strengthsfinder&utm_campaign=coming_soon&utm_medium=redirect
6. https://www.amazon.com/Crucial-Conversations-Tools-Talking-Stakes-ebook/dp/
   B000GCFEV2

And tell them what you want. Be very clear on your ask.

Tip #1. Keep an "Atta-Girl" file. Fill this file up with the wonderful things people say about you, the thanks they give you, and all that recognition you receive. Open it frequently to remind yourself how absolutely amazing and brilliant and wonderful and talented and beautiful you are.

<u>BONUS TIP</u>: Find your Voice. Use it for good. Be loud. Find allies. Be kind. And remember, rules are made to be broken.

> *If you obey all the rules, you miss all the fun.*
> ~ Katharine Hepburn

About Pat

Pat Obuchowski considers herself an unorthodox rational optimist. She is the CEO (Chief Empowerment Officer) of inVisionaria, a leadership development company. She helps her clients go from good to great by sharpening their leadership skills, interpersonal communication, and organizational skills. This helps them achieve their vision on a professional and personal level.

Pat helps leaders build strong and results-oriented teams by mastering their strengths, managing their weaknesses, and becoming skillful in using coaching skills to help others. She helps people create plans that inspire them and then coaches them in the implementation of those plans. She coaches for results.

Pat has worked with individuals and teams at for-profit organizations, such as Union Bank, Bayer, Hilton Worldwide, and Lockheed, and nonprofit organizations, such as FUSE Corps, American Red Cross, National Speaker's Association, and Kaiser Permanente. She served as a Principal and Leadership Development Partner and coach with Pacific Gas & Electric Company, where she coached corporate leaders and teams to be more impactful in their work and in the world, and helped them vision and play their Bigger Games.

Pat is the founder of *Gutsy Women Win* whose mission is to support women leaders around the world.

She is the author of the book *Gutsy Women Win: How to Get Gutsy and Get Going* that describes a model for success that helps readers identify their passions for leadership and life and then empowers them to pursue them. It offers the reader an opportunity to examine how the model works through the lens of the stories of seven game-changing women.

Pat also authored *Gutsy Leaders: 140 Bits of Wisdom on How to Build Great Teams with Vision and Compassion*; and is the co-author of *Scrappy Women in Business: Living Proof That Bending the Rules Isn't Breaking the Law.*

Pat is a public speaker, blogger, and workshop leader. She serves on the Forbes Coaching Council and is a contributing author on Forbes.com. In addition to post-graduate work in the Neuroscience of Leadership, she has her MBA and a BA in Psychology/Sociology. She is an International Coach Federation credentialed coach as well as a certified coach through Coaches Training Institute.

Pat is a world traveler who supports President Eisenhower's belief that "peaceful relations between nations requires understanding and mutual respect between individuals." She knows that travel allows one to acquire this understanding and respect when exchanging conversations with others outside of our home country. If we take the time to become engaged and knowledgeable about other cultures we will be an active force in creating a world that is more peaceful and respectful to each other.

Contact Pat directly at:
- Pat@inVisionaria.com

For more information:
- GutsyWomenWin.com
- https://www.linkedin.com/in/patobuchowski/
- Facebook.com/GutsyWomenWin
- Twitter.com/GutsyWomenWin
- Instagram.com/GutsyWomenWin

CHAPTER 23

TRANSFORMATIONAL LEADERSHIP: KNOWING YOUR *WHY* IS ESSENTIAL TO YOUR RESULTS

BY DR. AIMÉE V. SANCHEZ

The one principle that can lead to success in any area of business is for a leader to know their purpose. They must center on the "why."

In my own life, I have always considered myself somewhat pragmatic, logical, and laser-focused when it came to pursuing my goals. I connected the why in what I pursued to the actions I took. This focus from such a young age likely stemmed from familial ties and my cultural worldview, which was rooted in a strong sense of community and personal responsibility. Challenges in my childhood such as poverty, divorce, and lack of resources served as opportunities to excel and did not dissuade or deter me. Instead, they fueled my desire to transcend the limits of my personal reality. A life unfulfilled never seemed like it would be my destiny, mostly because I would not allow it. I knew exactly why I wanted to move past it and what that took.

I had a desire to strive for my own better way to live and to also help others achieve their best life.

My path toward self-exploration and investment in others led me to pursue the field of Psychology, and this is where I remain twenty years later. I work with individuals from diverse backgrounds who have encountered struggles and trials on their pathway to healing, transformation, and growth. It's a career that requires you have a heart for people, as well as a strategic plan of direction to guide them in. It's a healthy respect for the seriousness of life that has propelled me throughout my career to pursue the work – whatever it may be – with a sense of urgency.

What I've found to be very interesting through all of this is how this very discipline and understanding of my why is really the key for all people, especially in regard to those who strive for leadership roles. At the base level, we must be leaders in our own initiatives and at the corporate level, leadership is intricately linked to the results of the organization.

In the 2016 Workforce Purpose Index, they found that only 30% of US workers are engaged in their jobs. This means that two out of three workers are disengaged.

Studies like this are very revealing and helpful to me in my work as a Psychologist and Success Strategist. They show me that without the why in a corporate environment, the quality of the environment, and most likely the success of it, is in peril. A more holistic and transformational approach to leadership could make a profound difference, and it's my why in my work that I am doing with individuals and corporations. As a consultant, I am helping businesses achieve their purposes through ensuring their employees are engaged in their why – their passions.

Many people are just like I was when I was younger – enthusiastic, inspired, and passionate. However, they lose their connection to these valuable driving forces along the way. What I've discovered as I matured is that success is a moving target and can be relative, depending upon where your values and opinions originate about what success means. For some, success will appear to be material, measured by the vision of their ideal career, family, objects, cars, money in their bank accounts, etc. While, for others, success will be measured by a state of being and feeling on track with a specific life purpose.

For me, success has been balanced against the barometer of the individuals whom I was destined to touch. I have internalized success to mean that as long as I am moving in the direction of my God-given purpose and mission – along with others being blessed – then I am successful. Doing this means not losing sight of my purpose and always remembering my why. This is what I am so excited about today, and demonstrating the potential of this through meaningful action is the start to creating a cultural shift... one that may lead to two out of three workers being engaged to the ideal—all workers are engaged in their jobs—which equates to being engaged in their overall lives.

LEADERSHIP WITH PURPOSE
Developing our success and purpose is an ongoing process,
a lifelong journey that defines us.

One of the joys in working my field is seeing the evolution and transformation that takes place in the individual and organization once there is defined clarity. In my partnership with the John Maxwell Team, I have learned that leadership is influence, and that leaders must be dutiful in their responsibility to shape and guide others.

John Maxwell, who is an author, speaker, pastor, and trainer, has been one of the most influential leaders in my life and career. His leadership principles about success resonate so closely to my goals to develop why-driven leadership principles in the workplace. Maxwell talks about the three critical elements of success, which include:

1. Knowing your purpose in life.
2. Growing to reach your maximum potential.
3. Sowing seeds that benefit others.

These aspects of purpose are at the very heart of what a leader is— regardless of the number of people they lead or their position. They are all equally important and intricately intermingled. However, when they are put together they create a powerful transformation in a person's life which extends to all the environments they are in contact with—their homes, their work, and their social circles.

KNOWING YOUR PURPOSE IN LIFE

Purpose comes from the heart, the intuition, and our emotions. It moves us and others because we are moved by it. Through purpose we are more engaged and are able to generate an unstoppable level of personal power that will give us courage and resilience when necessary.

Without purpose, we are like a flickering candle
instead of a blazing light.

Through growth and development, a leader can leave a lasting impact on their team and be able to articulate their purpose in a transparent way. The result can be a pathway for the rest of the community to also learn and embrace their purpose. The collective effort is more consistent and it's also filled with enthusiasm. There is a saying that, "nothing great was ever achieved without passion." When you are starting to connect with your purpose in life the passion comes about naturally and you feel this energy that you are onto something big—not only for yourself, but for those around you, as well. For a business, this is powerful. It's the way of the future and an expectation for new entrants into the work force.

There was an article in June 2017 by Andrea Jacques of Kyosei Consulting, a firm specializing in work transformation, which stated, "Millennials have a different relationship to purpose than previous generations, with over 70% saying they value purpose at work. Though not all Millennials are of work-age yet, in a few years they will be the most represented generation in the workforce." This is important to grasp because while you may feel this type of transformation is hard – and rightfully so – it is unavoidable. And embracing it will enable stronger leadership qualities to preside.

GROWING TO REACH YOUR MAXIMUM POTENTIAL

Our maximum potential requires clarity... clarity of mission, of direction, of values. Furthermore, without clarity our motivations can be questioned and our pursuits jeopardized. No matter how much we may desire something or try, our efforts will be sabotaged if clarity is lacking, which means that we cannot achieve our maximum potential. On a leadership level, this type of ambiguity can be confusing for employees and cause a lack of engagement.

As a leader, you cannot avoid making decisions and the correlation to these decisions and your results is real. Will you make a mistake or two? Most likely, yes, but when you know your why, mistakes happen less and you keep moving toward your maximum potential more. It may seem complicated, but it is simple in theory.

With a clear purpose a leader can sieve through the barrage of options presented to him or her with more focus. They are attuned to what is required; therefore, they can send and receive the appropriate broadcast. They are the epitome of "what you send out, you will receive in return."

SOWING SEEDS THAT BENEFIT OTHERS

There's a wonderful quote by Tavis Smiley that resonates with me about the importance of sowing seeds that benefit others. Smiley says, "The choices we make about the lives we live determine the kinds of legacies we leave."

I believe that when you continue to sow the seeds that benefit others, you gain access to your true calling. It's critical for a leader to know their purpose because it makes them a better leader. When this mindset is in motion, you are not only navigating the course of your own life, but you are causing a chain reaction in which others will chart and navigate their own lives in a more authentic manner. As a leader, you've helped all members of your team realize their value by connecting with their why. It is in this symbiotic relationship between the success of a leader and that of the follower that we find the greater significance earlier referred to.

THE FIVE CHARACTERISTICS OF LEADERS WHO WALK IN PURPOSE

A leader is not defined by their words alone, but also by the actions they take to grow a purpose-driven, "why"-focused, work environment.

In my years of working with people and organizations seeking solutions, I have borne witness to transformations that are truly inspiring. It begins with the individual who has a passion that is suddenly sparked. Before long it's an ember and it just keeps growing, turning into energy that you are drawn to and energy that produces results. This is the ultimate goal for any leader who understands the value of those around them, whether their position is "above" or "below" theirs in the hierarchy of the organization.

Out of the many characteristics that define our destinies, there are five that are particularly important to a purposeful leader. These are what you need to evaluate if you are in a leadership position or aspire to be in one. What you do today can make a difference, starting today.

1. <u>You can choose to exude an excellent attitude.</u>
    It certainly seems obvious, but when we get caught up in the fray of life, our attitude is often the first thing to suffer. Having a positive and optimistic attitude is a non-negotiable for a purpose-driven leader. They know that a different perspective during a trying time can be the catalyst that leads to solving any problem, whether it's one of morale or a situation that impacts the flow of business.

2. <u>You understand the importance of credibility.</u>
    Through credibility, a stronger and more prosperous organization is created. When you are committed to building credibility it leads to trust within the organization. The choice of taking integrity over appearance, truth over convenience, and honor over self-motives is a powerful one. It's done through action – not words – and it leaves a footprint of credibility for others to follow in.

3. <u>You always look for the potential in others.</u>
    Whomever a leader may have influence over is someone they should want to achieve their fullest potential. This takes a commitment of time and a dedication to knowing that an organization is truly elevated when the individual knows that they are a person of value within it. This is where true innovation can take place because the person whose potential is recognized will contribute more to their organization.

4. <u>Your actions reveal inspired confidence.</u>
    As a leader, through belief in yourself and your abilities you will find you possess the clarity of vision, mindset, and purpose that demonstrates inspired confidence. Let's face it, when the leader lacks confidence, this reflects quickly downward. However, when the leader embodies confidence, it reassures others and allows for a pro-growth, solutions-based culture that has truly set itself up to excel. Be the leader who demonstrates the authentic, inspired confidence.

5. <u>You are a person with a service-based mindset.</u>
    Leaders are different than "bosses." They don't look at people and simply assign tasks to them based on a certain need. A leader is a servant first, realizing that a corporate culture begins with the natural feeling that one wants to serve those around them by being genuinely vested in the growth and wellbeing of those around them.

This mindset is a part of a leader's personal life philosophy and it shows through their words and actions on a continual basis.

A transformational leader is someone who has the power to modify the beliefs and attitudes of the employees by inspiring them. They don't want to change them to fit "their mold." They simply want to help all those around them in an organization connect with their why.

Purpose-driven leaders show a positive attitude and act in a way that allows them to be of service as they inspire those around them and help to reveal their team's fullest potential.

Whether you are a leader today, aspiring to be one, or are a person of influence, you have the ability to take on the qualities that will make you the purpose-driven leader, a person of great integrity and inspiration to the world around you. This is your destiny and the journey to it is transformational.

About Dr. Sanchez

Dr. Aimée V. Sanchez is a Psychologist, and Certified John Maxwell Team Executive Coach, Speaker, and Trainer who has specialized in Neuropsychology and Organizational/Business consulting for the last 17 years. The Organizational Consulting & Leadership Development component of her practice is devoted to a holistic transformational approach to leadership.

Through the years of her recognized corporate career, Dr. Sanchez has served in various capacities, in executive, staff, and support-level positions. All of these have enabled her to gain a wide range of leadership experiences including, but not limited to: Strategic Operations, Operational Planning, Leadership Development and Training, Human Resources, Employee Retention, Conflict Management, Recruiting and Applicant Screening, Project and Budget Management, Finance Accountability, Sales, Customer Service, Compliance, and Marketing. Her expertise extends to use of Neurolinguistic Programming (NLP), Psychology and evidenced- based practices to help individuals develop and implement strategies that will enhance their personal and professional effectiveness.

Dr. Sanchez has been mentored by some of the most prominent thought leaders in the industry including John Maxwell, and she is extremely passionate about helping to develop the maximum human potential that all people possess. Today, Dr. Sanchez is also a Best-Selling Author with Jack Canfield – the #1 Success Coach in America – having contributed a chapter to his book *Success Starts Today*. Dr. Sanchez specializes in Executive & Success Coaching and Business Transformation. She is also a motivational speaker and Best-Selling author of her 2017 book titled, *Disrupt The Status Quo: Living and Leading From Your Success Zone.*

Despite having much of her career centered in the corporate realm, Dr. Sanchez has shared that her inspiration for working with those in the area of transformational change comes from her innate passion to catapult others growth to reach their maximum potential. She states, "I want to empower individuals to not only transform themselves, but others around them; whether it be in the work place (with their teams and organizations) or in their personal life (with their families and in their communities). I believe 'transformed lives' transform lives."

Dr. Sanchez spends a large amount of her time pouring into others through coaching, mentoring others, and training. She utilizes her relevant industry expertise and acumen to help others become successful. Her methodologies are measurable and effective; her keynote speeches and training sessions leave participants with motivation to take action and pursue their optimal potential. She maintains a passion and belief in experiential trainings that are meaningful to the participant and are critical in the facilitation of holistic transformational leaps in vital areas of life, including professional, financial, relationships, spiritual, health, personal growth, and community investment.

Dr. Sanchez resides with her husband and their two children in California. In her spare time, she enjoys travel, singing, listening to music, and spending time with her family.

Connect with Dr. Sanchez at:
- Email: avsanchezphd@gmail.com
- Website: www.dravsanchez.com
- LinkedIn: https://www.linkedin.com/in/aimee-v-sanchez-ph-d-26a355141/

CHAPTER 24

HOW TO MAKE A DIFFERENCE: BE THE CHANGE

BY GABI LASZINGER

We all have a definition of "purpose." For some people, it means making an impact on the world. For others, it refers to a calling – anywhere between a skill or an industry. In reality, many of us get caught up in the rat race of career and ambition, thinking that all of the answers lie in paychecks or other measures of success. Our achievements can even fall flat once we have them: we are then apt to desire new things, or we don't feel like they are enough.

That was me, 20 years ago. At this point I had already accomplished so much, rising up from absolute poverty in Yugoslavia, to my youth in Germany. You could say mine was already a success story: I was determined from a young age to ascend class and educate myself. I fought relentlessly to get to where I was, as I experienced hard impacts of life first-hand – from outcast immigrants (my parents) to judgement as a teen mother (myself). I climbed the proverbial ladder and worked hard, because I believed that achieving wealth and success would equal happiness.

So, it was somewhat surprising to find myself in the position of having much with something still missing. I knew what being poor felt like; but this was more like a poverty of the soul. Professionally, I was a highly successful and well-known coach and spiritual teacher, working with CEOs and clients who relied on me. My needs were being met with physical goods – I had a roof over my head, and a comfortable balance in my bank account.

What I would come to learn is that you must also be in tune with your purpose for it to be enough. Life either destroys you or teaches you, and I decided at a young age that I would not be torn down that easily. Therefore . . .

- I learned from people who let me down -- what trust is.
- I learned from people who rejected me -- what strength is.
- I learned from people who stopped caring -- what love is.

I invite you to take steps towards finding your own true purpose. And what I learned was vital: when you find a way to help others, you help yourself along the way.

Before we dig in, let's start with a quick exercise. Close your eyes. Forget your bills or that unfinished project in your closet. Imagine you had time and resources, and the incredible opportunity to use them infinitely for one month. Step outside of yourself and think about the world around you. Where would you step in to help for those 30 days, if you had the privilege to do so? What has always resonated with you? Hold that thought as you read on.

MY ROCK BOTTOM

Eighteen years ago, I was searching for the "meaning of life" as a backpacker in the Himalayan kingdom of Nepal. I thought I'd call upon the wise teachers of India and Nepal for guidance. Nepal is a land of extremes. The terrain is vast and varied, from low-lying jungles to stunning snow-capped mountains. Like the land, the social landscape has highs and lows, from wealth to poverty. In Nepal, the caste system determines a person's worth even before birth.

My inner voice was trying to break through, but I never quite got the message. Instead, I had a lot of doubt and sadness. I was constantly thinking, "Who am I? What am I doing? Do I matter?" I acknowledge that I was doing better than my family before me, yet I was hopelessly lost. Wasn't money and achievement enough? Was I simply ungrateful? Surely, I was doing something wrong. How could life be so hard and unfulfilling? Despite my successes, I was unhappy and lost, and believing I was not making any impact on the world in a measurable way.

This is how I came to spend time in the Himalayas. You name it, I tried it: ceremonies with shamans, praying with holy men and women, covering myself in white ashes, chanting mantras with monks on mountain tops. I couldn't relax. I never achieved Nirvana. I did not feel strong, good, or useful. I was wringing myself out like a wet towel, but there was nothing left to drain out.

After all this searching, I never realized that I was part of my own problem. Which is to say, even though I was working as a coach helping many people become self-aware and find themselves . . . an awareness was missing inside of me, and I couldn't access it. I was blind to the bigger things around me that really mattered. It made me feel humble, small, and most importantly: I felt like I had a place to be and grow.

A TURNING POINT

Sometimes, you find what you're most in need of while out looking for something else. My turning point happened after getting lost, walking the narrow old streets of Kathmandu. Through backyards and old temples, I got turned around, then receded further and further into unfamiliar territory.

It was there that I lost my way, although in hindsight, perhaps this is where I was "found."

The streets were filthy, and the air smelled from all the garbage everywhere. There was blood from the slaughtered buffalo killed alongside the muddy banks of the river. I remember thinking that nothing was sacred or holy in places of deep poverty, not even the holy river in which people worshipped. How could anyone live there? How could anyone be enlightened or saved here?

Around me were many children who begged with hungry eyes. My gaze was drawn to three children who were somehow different. They wore only rags and were dirty. When I took a closer look, I noticed that they were full of lice and parasites, with wounds on their heads. My heart sunk in a way only a parent can understand.

I'd later learn there were hundreds of children in this condition all over Nepal. I was so lost and preoccupied searching for my own enlightenment that I almost lost touch with the humanity all around me. Almost. All I had to do was meet the gaze of these three little boys.

The oldest boy, Ashik, was 7 years old and shy. He seemed genuinely embarrassed to be begging, his hands outstretched for himself and his two brothers. Ashok, the middle one, was just 5 years old, but could hardly stand on his feet. Weak and timid, he reached his hands out as well. The smallest one, Abinash, was a baby boy: an infant lying on plastic, wearing only an ill-fitted shirt. I was in shock, but I didn't hesitate: I needed to do something. I first gave them some sips of my water, but that wasn't enough. I immediately went out in search of food for them, and came back with something I thought to be very special (especially for children): a hamburger. I'll never forget how they looked at it, so puzzled; they didn't know what this strange, round thing was, let alone how to eat it.

My thoughts were heavy when I went back to the hotel that night: I could not let go of all these impressions, as I tried to make sense of what I had seen, and strategize about what I could do.

The next day, I went back to that same place hoping to see them again. The fate of the boys had seized me. From a distance, I saw the youngest one lying lifelessly on the ground. My heart beat fast, and I panicked, assuming the worst.

It's well documented that people have moments of adrenaline and super-human strength: our fight or flight. After a moment, the little one moved again. I made the decision to stop thinking and act, and immediately ran to him. When I did this, it forever changed me in an instant. In this moment, I could have overcome each and every difficulty, whatever it took to keep them alive.

There is a point where you know that you must do something. Perhaps you hesitate, because you don't feel strong or able enough, or maybe you don't know exactly what to do. It happens before you know it: suddenly something gives way, and you know that something must be done and the question of what just gives way to action, whatever it is, as long as it begins.

For me, I had to give up on the idea of saving myself first. Everything began with these three boys: I credit them for changing my life. It was like breathing oxygen for the first time. I saw how I could influence big changes. I felt energized, electric. But by saving others, I ended up saving myself.

YOUR PIVOT

A wrong attitude is a like a flat tire. If you don't change it, you don't go anywhere.

- What will be your turning point?
- How can you jumpstart it into action?
- How can you start today?

Acknowledging that it is daunting, and sometimes it even feels impossible to know how to apply this to our busy lives, is a fine first step in taking action. It means you are thinking, paying attention! Remember you can (and must!) start somewhere, and do more when the opportunities arise (and there will always be opportunities).

Maybe you have always wanted to help out in some ways, but have never made time. Start by thinking of opportunities that already resonate with you. For example, you may have always wanted to work with the elderly or a homeless shelter in your community. You may also discover that as soon as you start looking for possibilities, they materialize quite unexpectedly. Always take the opportunities that arise. You will never regret it.

--oo0Ooo--

My organization, Happy Children Trust, Nepal, is a certified non-profit charitable organization. We began in 1999 with those three little boys, and now support more than 200 children and many young mothers/fathers in Nepal out of child marriages. Our facility strives for self-sufficiency, so we grow our own fruits and vegetables, maintain livestock, and even have access to solar power.

We have only locals on staff. They are mostly uneducated, illiterate, unskilled. We believe that what this opportunity provides is invaluable to the organization as well as to these men and women: it reinforces all of our beliefs and extends the arm of making a difference. By showing them how much we trust in their abilities, suddenly they become strong, they develop skills, they develop a personality. This is part of the process of supporting an individual: just by showing them what we think they can achieve, they learn to believe in it for themselves.

We let all children stay until they are ready to be out in the world, which can mean through early vocational training or higher education. To us, it is important that they trust the foundation we are providing for them, and build strong roots.

Despite the difficulty we've faced during the 18 years doing this work, it has been immeasurably successful and rewarding. We are literally saving lives every day, and this is our goal that extends as a gift to touch others.

--ooOOoo--

Remember that question from earlier in the chapter? What was the thing that resonated with you? Where and how might you step up to help for those 30 days, if you had the privilege to do so?

We grow up believing that we must first love ourselves before loving others, and there is truth to that. However, it gives us a reason to procrastinate when we could be putting ourselves out there to support our community. These days, you find many people "navel-gazing": trying to find themselves in self-help seminars or wellness retreats, but lacking plans for greatness, or commitment to help their fellow man. Thoughts like "I have to get myself started first, I have to fill my account, buy my car, buy my house and feel good, love myself first, to be able to be there for others." These buy us the time we believe we need to begin. I'm here to tell you, you begin when you must.

You are so much stronger than you know, and our time on this Earth is fleeting. Regrets and procrastination do not serve us well when life begins to pass us by. If I could do anything differently in my life, I would have started helping sooner, but I am grateful for the opportunity to have this understanding now.

Maybe I wasn't Gandhi, Martin Luther King or Mother Theresa, but one thing I realized: if you save other people, you save the world, and you save yourself. When you make an effort and touch other people's lives, the world benefits. Your life has purpose. You walk taller. You find other ways of connecting and improving. It is a true giving cycle.

FINDING YOUR PURPOSE: FIVE WAYS TO BEGIN

Here are five steps you can use to jumpstart your own change. Think of the impact you can have if you begin now, instead of giving in to procrastination. It's always better to start now and make changes later.

1. Purge Selfish Thinking. The aspects of our personality that protect and serve us can also make us nearsighted.
2. Find your strength. It comes from within, and you are enough. Self-doubt is only human, don't let it drag you down.
3. Get Involved. Put the needs of others first and find ways to give without taking.
4. Do something bold. Taking risks is how some of the most inspiring and accomplished people you know make a difference in the world. Connect to your purpose by trying new things.
5. Worry about what comes next later. You don't need all the answers now, it is more important that you begin.

Reflect back here when you're feeling disconnected from the bigger picture, or need an extra push in the right direction.

ONE FINAL LESSON. . . FROM GRANDMA

To find your own purpose and connecting with the world around you, sometimes you just have to look around. My grandmother was a very humble and big-hearted woman, who was endlessly giving although she had almost nothing herself. I can still remember climbing onto her lap one night and asking, "Why, did you give the soup away to the beggars in the street when it was all you had for dinner tonight?"

She smiled gently and told me the words I still repeat. She told me, "Life means nothing if you don't live it for the good of others." Of course, as a child, I did not fully understand. Now, I understand that this is the only way to achieve happiness: *in the support of others.*

Start simple. Start with intentionality in every moment. Start with your good heart, even in the toughest business or circumstance. You never ever know how and when you will touch other people's lives. This is what the key is to your own change, change you didn't even realize you needed, but here it is.

About Gabi

Gabi Laszinger is a dynamic and empathic leader and who has positively influenced the lives of thousands of people. She has devoted her life to the support of others, especially those less fortunate. Her life's work and greatest passion project was the creation of her foundation, Happy Children Trust, Nepal.

Gabi's early years were spent in Yugoslavia, the child of Yugoslavian-Hungarian parents. Throughout their lives, they experienced poverty and discrimination. Her family struggled to make ends meet and experienced injustices and prejudice based on their background and class. Yet it was observing her family's struggle that set Laszinger on a determined path to improve her circumstances and never give up. She lives her life by the motto: "We are all strong, we just do not know how strong we are."

Laszinger's professional work falls into two major chapters. The first chapter was a prosperous career as a life coach, spiritual teacher, speaker, and hypnotist. In the mid-1990s, another chapter began, as her life took a turn which redefined everything for Gabi. While on a spiritual quest, she had a clandestine encounter with three starving young boys in Nepal in 1999. She speaks openly about how this interaction changed her life and path in the blink of an eye, and acknowledges that there was no way to return home and forget the misery of what she saw.

Her second and current chapter is the creation of a non-profit humanitarian effort known as Happy Children (www.happy-children.de) after she gave up everything in her "old" life. Today, Happy Children is a two-facility orphanage, home for over 200 children and a staff of 50 in the Himalayas. This organization has changed the lives of hundreds of people and continues to do important work under Laszinger's leadership and support.

Though Gabi Laszinger prefers doing her work privately without much media or attention, she has much to be proud of, including receiving the Presidential Medal of Freedom. Her orphanage, Happy Children Trust, was also awarded the South-East Asia's Best Architectural Project.

Gabi Laszinger hopes by sharing her story, and as an advocate for humanitarian and social justice work, she can influence others to connect with their true calling and make a difference in the world. She wholeheartedly believes that a single person can change a lot, if they believe in it. Her primary goal is to show people what ethics, morals and humanity means, in order to make a real change over generations.

CPSIA information can be obtained
at www.ICGtesting.com
Printed in the USA
BVOW09*0748160418
513498BV00004B/16/P

9 780999 171417